First World War
and Army of Occupation
War Diary
France, Belgium and Germany

34 DIVISION
102 Infantry Brigade
Cheshire Regiment
1/4th Battalion.
20 January 1918 - 22 March 1919

WO95/2462/1

The Naval & Military Press Ltd
www.nmarchive.com
Published in association with The National Archives

Published by

The Naval & Military Press Ltd

Unit 10 Ridgewood Industrial Park,

Uckfield, East Sussex,

TN22 5QE England

Tel: +44 (0) 1825 749494

www.naval-military-press.com

www.nmarchive.com

This diary has been reprinted in facsimile from the original. Any imperfections are inevitably reproduced and the quality may fall short of modern type and cartographic standards.

© Crown Copyright
Images reproduced by permission of The National Archives, London, England, 2015.

Contents

Document type	Place/Title	Date From	Date To
Heading	34th Division 102nd Infy Bde 1-4th Bn Cheshire Regt. 1918 Jly-1919 Mar To 1 Div (Raine Army) From Egypt 53 Div 159 Bde		
War Diary	Hoflande	01/07/1918	07/07/1918
War Diary	Schools Camp	08/07/1918	13/07/1918
War Diary	Cormette Camp	04/07/1918	15/07/1918
War Diary	Hoflande	16/07/1918	16/07/1918
War Diary	En Route	17/07/1918	17/07/1918
War Diary	Fontaine	18/07/1918	19/07/1918
War Diary	Vez	20/07/1918	20/07/1918
War Diary	Puiseux	21/07/1918	22/07/1918
War Diary	Oulchy Le Chateau 1/20000 771.847	22/07/1918	23/07/1918
War Diary	Oulchy Le Chateau 1/2000	23/07/1918	31/07/1918
Miscellaneous	Casualty Return Month Ending	31/07/1918	31/07/1918
War Diary	Map Oulchy Le Chateau 1/20,000	01/08/1918	04/08/1918
War Diary	Silly Le Long	05/08/1918	05/08/1918
War Diary	Le Plessis Belleville	06/08/1918	06/08/1918
War Diary	Zeggers Cappel	07/08/1918	12/08/1918
War Diary	Herzeele	13/08/1918	18/08/1918
War Diary	Herzeele Map Sheet 27	19/08/1918	19/08/1918
War Diary	Penton Camp. Proven	20/08/1918	20/08/1918
War Diary	Penton Camp. Proven Ref Map Sheets 27.28 1/20.000	21/08/1918	21/08/1918
War Diary	Brake Camp. Ref. Map. Sheet 28 1/2000 A.30.C.	22/08/1918	22/08/1918
War Diary	Brake Camp A.30.c Sheet 28 1/2000	23/08/1918	24/08/1918
War Diary	Arrival Farm Sheet 28 B.2.8.d.5.3	27/08/1918	27/08/1918
War Diary	Road Camp	27/08/1918	28/08/1918
War Diary	Cormette Camp.	29/08/1918	31/08/1918
Miscellaneous	Brief account of Operations from 22nd July to 2nd August, 1918	09/08/1918	09/08/1918
Miscellaneous	1/4th Batt. Cheshire Regiment. Operation Order. No. 1	12/08/1918	12/08/1918
Operation(al) Order(s)	1/4th Battalion The Cheshire Regiment Operation Order No. 2	18/08/1918	18/08/1918
War Diary	Cormette	01/09/1918	01/09/1918
War Diary	Lumbres	01/09/1918	01/09/1918
War Diary	Scherpenberg	02/09/1918	02/09/1918
War Diary	Vierstraat Switch	03/09/1918	09/09/1918
War Diary	Scherpenberg	10/09/1918	15/09/1918
War Diary	Line	15/09/1918	22/09/1918
War Diary	Scherpenberg	23/09/1918	30/09/1918
Heading	1/4th Bn The Cheshire Regiment. War Diary October 1918 Vol 5		
War Diary	Wytchaete	01/10/1918	03/10/1918
War Diary	Reference Map Sheet 28 1/40,000	04/10/1918	12/10/1918
War Diary	Field. Reference Map Sheet 28 1/40000	13/10/1918	19/10/1918
War Diary	Field. She Anne Reference Map Sheet 28 1/40.000	20/10/1918	26/10/1918
War Diary	Field Ref. Map Sheet 28 1/40.000	27/10/1918	31/10/1918
Miscellaneous	Casualty Return	31/10/1918	31/10/1918
Heading	1/4th Bn The Cheshire Regt. War Diary Appendix No. 1		

Type	Description	Start	End
Miscellaneous	1/4th Bn The Cheshire Regt. War Diary Appendix No. 1	01/10/1918	01/10/1918
Miscellaneous	1/4th Bn The Cheshire Regt. War Diary Appendix No. 2		
Miscellaneous	1/4th Bn The Cheshire Regt. War Diary Appendix No. 2	11/10/1918	11/10/1918
Heading	1/4 Bn The Cheshire Regt. War Diary Appendix No. 3		
Miscellaneous	1/4th Bn The Cheshire Regt. War Diary Appendix No. 3	16/10/1918	16/10/1918
Heading	1/4th Bn The Cheshire Regt. War Diary Appendix No. 4		
Miscellaneous	1/4th Bn The Cheshire Regt. War Diary Appendix No. 4	15/10/1918	15/10/1918
Heading	1/4th Bn The Cheshire Regt. War Diary Appendix No. 5 Oct		
Miscellaneous	1/4th Bn The Cheshire Regt. War Diary Appendix No. 5	23/10/1918	23/10/1918
Operation(al) Order(s)	Addition to Operation Order No. 3	24/10/1918	24/10/1918
Heading	1/4th Bn The Cheshire Regt. War Diary Appendix No. 6		
Miscellaneous	1/4th Bn The Cheshire Regt. War Diary Appendix No. 6	24/10/1918	24/10/1918
Heading	1/4th Bn The Cheshire Regt. War Diary Appendix No. 7		
Miscellaneous	1/4th Bn The Cheshire Regt. War Diary Appendix No. 7	25/10/1918	25/10/1918
War Diary	Narlebeke	01/11/1918	06/11/1918
War Diary	Sheet 29 1/40,000	07/11/1918	12/11/1918
War Diary	Moorseele	13/11/1918	14/11/1918
War Diary	Belleghem	15/11/1918	15/11/1918
War Diary	Celles	16/11/1918	18/11/1918
War Diary	La Pierre	19/11/1918	25/11/1918
War Diary	Flobecq	26/11/1918	30/11/1918
Miscellaneous	Summary of Casualties Reinforcements During Nove 1918		
War Diary	Flobecq	01/12/1918	12/12/1918
War Diary	Chislenghien	13/12/1918	14/12/1918
War Diary	Soignies	15/12/1918	20/12/1918
War Diary	Vitrival	21/12/1918	27/12/1918
War Diary	Vitrival And Aisemont	28/12/1918	31/12/1918
Heading	1/4 Cheshire Regt 1919 Jan-1919 Mar		
War Diary	Vitrival & Aisemont	01/01/1919	19/01/1919
War Diary	(Namur 1/10.0000)	20/01/1918	23/01/1918
War Diary	(Germany 1/100.000)	24/01/1919	31/01/1919
Miscellaneous	Summary of Casualties For Month of January 1919		
War Diary	Lind Germany	01/03/1919	23/03/1919
War Diary	Roisdorf	23/03/1919	27/03/1919
War Diary	Hersel And Roisdorf	28/03/1919	31/03/1919
Miscellaneous	Casualties	31/03/1919	31/03/1919
Miscellaneous	1/4 Bn Cheshire Regt. Training Programme Week Ending 8/3/19	08/03/1919	08/03/1919
Miscellaneous	1/4 Bn Cheshire Regt. Training Programme Week Ending 15/3/19	15/03/1919	15/03/1919
War Diary	1/4 Bn Cheshire Regt. Training Programme Week Ending 22/3/19	22/03/1919	22/03/1919

34TH DIVISION
102ND INFY BDE BEF FRANCE

1-4TH BN CHESHIRE REGT.
~~JUN~~ JULY – DEC 1918

1918 JLY — 1919 MAR

TO 1 DIV (RHINE ARMY)

FROM EGYPT 53 DIV / 159 BDE

+ 2/8t Tyneside Irishmen NF

WAR DIARY
or
INTELLIGENCE SUMMARY.
(Erase heading not required.)

1/4 BN THE CHESHIRE

Place	Date	Hour	Summary of Events and Information	
HOFLANDE	1/7/15		Day spent cleaning & straightening up after train journey	JB
do.	2/7/15	6 am to 7 am / 8.30 to 12.30	Gas training. All Coys. Training musketry, Lewis Gun, Signallers & Scouts, all Companies & Bn. H.Q.	JB
do.	3/7/15	6 am to 7 am / 8.30 to 12.30	Gas training all Coys. Bn. H.Q. Training musketry &c &c. G.O.C. 3rd Divn. would inspect Baths. Warning received that G.O.C. 3rd Divn. would inspect Baths.	JB
do.	4/7/15	10.30 / 11.30	Baths. Paraded for I.O.C.'s inspection. G.O.C. 3rd Divn. inspected the Baths & congratulated them on their turnout.	JB
do.	5/7/15	6 am to 7 am / 8.30 / 12.30	Gas training. All Coys. & H.Q. Training musketry Lewis Guns &c.	JB

Army Form C. 2118.

WAR DIARY
or
INTELLIGENCE SUMMARY.

(Erase heading not required.)

Instructions regarding War Diaries and Intelligence
Summaries are contained in F. S. Regs., Part II.
and the Staff Manual respectively. Title pages
will be prepared in manuscript.

Place	Date	Hour	Summary of Events and Information	Remarks and references to Appendices
HOFLANDE	6/7/18	6 am 7 am 7.30 12.30	Training Gen. All Coys other HQ. do Musketry, L.G. etc. do do do Orders received that Battn. would move to SCHOOLS CAMP tomorrow.	SS
HOFLANDE	7/7/18	10 am 11 am 1.30 pm	Batln. Parade ready to move to SCHOOLS CAMP Batln. from starting point. Batln. arrived at SCHOOLS CAMP. Warned that Coy's Coyhr & army would in whole Battalion.	SS
SCHOOLS CAMP	8/7/18	6 am 10, 11, 12 noon 2 pm 2.4 pm	Divisional Baths at disposal of Battalion. Baths allotted to Coys for 1 hour each. Musketry, Bayonet Fighting, & Lewis Gun. Training on 30 yds. Range. Grouping practices.	SS
do.	9/7/18	9.20 10.30 12.15.	Battalion Parade for inspection by G.O.C. Coyhr & Army. Inspection. G.O.C. expressed himself highly satisfied with turnout of the Battalion. G.O.C. II Corps. spoke to all Officers of the Battalion.	SS

Army Form C. 2118.

WAR DIARY
or
INTELLIGENCE SUMMARY.
(Erase heading not required.)

Instructions regarding War Diaries and Intelligence Summaries are contained in F. S. Regs., Part II. and the Staff Manual respectively. Title pages will be prepared in manuscript.

Place	Date	Hour	Summary of Events and Information	Remarks and references to Appendices
SCHOOLS CAMP	9/7/16		Orders received that Brigade would carry out a practice occupation of trenches in the EAST POPERINGHE defence line, the Battalion to occupy right SECTOR NO.1.	
		5pm	Operation Orders Brigade Everson No.1. received.	
		7pm	Battn. Orders with reference to Bde. Everson No.1. issued (copy attached)	JP
		10.20.	Battalion moved out of SCHOOLS CAMP in accordance with above orders	
		12.10	Occupation of entire SECTOR reported complete.	
		2pm 2.30 am	Orders received to march back to CAMP.	
		3.40	Battalion arrived in CAMP.	
do.	10/7/16	11am to 4pm	Training. All troops. Musketry, Practices on Zeyu RANGE. Bayonet fighting. Lewis Gun. Practice on 30 yds. RANGE.	JP
do.	11/7/16	8am to 11am 2pm 4pm	Training All troops. Musketry. Practices on Zeyu RANGE. Lewis Gun. do. Bayonet fighting, including Special Class for N.C.O's under instructor. A.J.S.	JP

D. D. & L., London, E.C. (A8004) W. W7771/M2/31 750,000 5/17 Sch: 52 Forms/C2118/14.

WAR DIARY
or
INTELLIGENCE SUMMARY.

(Erase heading not required.)

Army Form C. 2118.

Instructions regarding War Diaries and Intelligence Summaries are contained in F. S. Regs., Part II. and the Staff Manual respectively. Title pages will be prepared in manuscript.

Place	Date	Hour	Summary of Events and Information	Remarks and references to Appendices
SCHOOLS CAMP.	12/7/15	8 am 6.12 am 2.30 pm 6.4.30	Testing of S.B.R's. All S.B.R's tested & whole of Battalion passed through Gas Chamber. Carried out under supervision of Divisional Gas Officer. Time not spent on this. Cleaning & scratching at Disposal Baths. Orders received for move tomorrow to CORMETTE MUSKETRY CAMP and Entraining party sent in.	JB
do.	13/7/15	7.6 am 11 am 11 am 2.30 pm 6 pm 5.15 pm	Transport moved to CORMETTE MUSKETRY CAMP by march route. Battalion left SCHOOLS CAMP for PROVEN do. Arrived PROVEN STATION. Entrained do. Detrained ST. OMER. and marched to CORMETTE CAMP Arrived CORMETTE CAMP.	JB
CORMETTE CAMP	14/7/15	5 am to 9 am	Ranges allotted to the Battalion during their hours for musketry. Whole Battalion carried out application practices at 200 yds.	JB
do.	15/7/15	9 am to 1 pm	Ranges allotted to the Battalion during their hours. Ranges allotted for Practices carried out. Application 200yds. with cover do without cover.	JB

WAR DIARY
or
INTELLIGENCE SUMMARY.

Army Form C. 2118.

Place	Date	Hour	Summary of Events and Information	Remarks and references to Appendices
CORMETTE CAMP	15/7/18	11.15 am	Orders received that Battalion was to be ready to move at short notice. Range practices abandoned, & orders to stand by issued.	
		11.30	Orders received that Transport would move at 12.30pm by march route to HOFLANDE.	
		12.30	Transport moved off at this hour.	
		1.15pm	Orders received for dismounted portion of Battalion to entrain at ST OMER at 4.30pm.	
		2.45pm	Battalion marched off starting point arrived ST OMER	
		6.30	do do entrained for RUSSEBRUGGE	
		5pm	do do entrained RUSSEBRUGGE and marched to HOFLANDE	
		8.45pm	do de Returned HOFLANDE and billeted	
		10.45pm	arrived	
HOFLANDE	16/7/18	5.15am	Orders received for entrainment at REXPODE. ons company with cooker to to entrain for train leaving at	
		2.50pm	Remainder of Battalion to entrain on 5.50pm train.	
		11.50am	"C" Coy. left HOFLANDE to entrain at REXPODE arrived 1.20pm.	
		3pm	A.B.D Coys & Batt H.Q. left HOFLANDE to entrain REXPODE arrived 4 rehr.	
		5.30pm	Entrainment of Battalion complete. Night spent on train	

Army Form C. 2118.

WAR DIARY
or
INTELLIGENCE SUMMARY.
(Erase heading not required.)

Instructions regarding War Diaries and Intelligence Summaries are contained in F. S. Regs., Part II. and the Staff Manual respectively. Title pages will be prepared in manuscript.

Place	Date	Hour	Summary of Events and Information	Remarks and references to Appendices
EN ROUTE	17/7/16	4.30pm 17/7/16 4.30am 11.30am	Spent on Train. Detrained at CHANTILLY & marched to FONTAINE. Battalion arrived FONTAINE & billeted.	
FONTAINE	18/7/16	11.30am	Whole day spent cleaning & washing. Battalion to be in readiness to move at short notice. Warning order to move received from of Employing to be notified later, batln. to be ready to move at 1hr. notice.	
FONTAINE	19/7/16	5.15am 6pm 6.45pm 12.30	Orders received for Battalion to embus at 6pm. Battalion started embussing, completed by 6.30pm. Transport moved off by road in accordance with march table. CAPTAIN K.S. CHANDLER and details remand to come on later. Battalion arrived VEZ and billeted. Orders received that Battalion be ready to move at half hours notice.	

Army Form C. 2118.

WAR DIARY
or
INTELLIGENCE SUMMARY.
(Erase heading not required.)

Instructions regarding War Diaries and Intelligence Summaries are contained in F. S. Regs., Part II. and the Staff Manual respectively. Title pages will be prepared in manuscript.

Place	Date	Hour	Summary of Events and Information	Remarks and references to Appendices
VEZ	20/7/16		Orders received for Battalion to remain in state of preparedness to move at half hours notice.	
		10.45 p.m.	Orders to move received. Batt. to move first starting point at 11.40 p.m.	
		noon	Head of Battalion passed starting point, continued march through night.	
PUISEUX	21/7/16	5.30 a.m.	Battalion arrived PUISEUX & billeted. Orders to move at short notice still applying. Day spent resting & cleaning.	
		5 p.m.	Warning orders for move on 22 inst. Kent received & Kinty sent out to reconnoitre route.	
		12 p.m.	Orders for march to LONGPONT received.	
PUISEUX	22/7/16	8.30 a.m.	Battalion moves to LONGPONT having starting point at 8.30 a.m. Arrived LONGPONT 3 p.m. & rested till 9.30 p.m.	
		9.30 p.m.	Battalion moved out to take over from the FRENCH REGT.	

WAR DIARY
or
INTELLIGENCE SUMMARY.

(Erase heading not required.)

Army Form C. 2118.

Instructions regarding War Diaries and Intelligence Summaries are contained in F. S. Regs., Part II. and the Staff Manual respectively. Title pages will be prepared in manuscript.

Place	Date	Hour	Summary of Events and Information	Remarks and references to Appendices
OULCHY LE CHATEAU Wood 771.847	22/7/18	11.50	Relief complete & Battalion in position reported to 102nd Inf Bde. Headquarters at Bois de Reploiries OULCHY (room). Batn. H.Q. 771.847. R.D.P. 766.846. "A" Coy 751.865, "B" Coy 777.865, "C" 774.846, "D" Coy. 769.865. 2 sections M.G. attached at 772.886.	
		12.00	Warning Orders for attack received	
do.	23/7/18	8.30	102nd Infantry Brigade Order No. 227 received (attached) and Plan of attack (attached)	
		5.15	1/4 Bn. Lancashire Regt. Operation Order No. 2, and Plan of Attack received (attached)	
		7.40 am	Orders for delivery of attack received. moved to position in tully at 830.450, arriving at this position at about 8 am. Remained in this position until 8.40 when enemy shelling became heavy. 8.40 continued advance to Trenches just N.E. of PARCY TIGNY. The Right Company ("C") moving into PARCY TIGNY. 9.30 Advance of leading Battalion seemed to be held up. The two	

WAR DIARY
or
INTELLIGENCE SUMMARY.

Army Form C. 2118.

Place	Date	Hour	Summary of Events and Information	Remarks and references to Appendices
OULCHY LE CHATEAU 1/100,000	23/7/18		Left Companies ("A" & "D") started to continue advance in direction of BOIS DE REUGNY, coming under very heavy M.G. fire from TIGNY. Their left flank was entirely exposed & they moved gradually over to their right into dead ground at about 93.44. Wrong in that position at about 10.30 am. "B" bty of the same times advanced their line to positions on trenches immediately E of PARCY-TIGNY. From 11.30 to 11.50 Companies reported their positions as follows. "A" Coy 178.200 to 286.200. "D" Coy on ROAD EAST of junction of road this SOUTH of hyphen in PARCY-TIGNY. "B" Coy Trenches about the "C" in PARCY-TIGNY. "C" Coy sunken road about S7.45. There "D" in PARCY-TIGNY. Battalion H.Q. about S7.45. from TIGNY leading boys were under heavy M.G. fire from TIGNY & dug in on last mentioned positions. their boys were also subjected to heavy artillery fire. The situation	R.B.

WAR DIARY
or
INTELLIGENCE SUMMARY.

Army Form C. 2118.

Place	Date	Hour	Summary of Events and Information	Remarks and references to Appendices

BULNY LE CHATEAU 1/20,000	23/7/18		Remained the same until about 9 pm. At this time orders were received to advance the line at dusk. Verbal Orders were issued to Coy Commanders and the line was advanced to the following positions about 10.0 pm "C" Coy from 00.42 to 00.45 "B" Coy from 97.42 to 97.45 A & D Coys 95.42 to 95.45. Battalion HQ in same position. The position was consolidated with the 1/f Cheshire Regt on the right. The right flank of the FRENCH UNIT on our left was at CROSS ROADS 88.48. The front was actively patrolled during the night. Casualties mostly due to heavy MG & Artillery fire, also Gas.
			
			                Killed Wounded Missing(Gas)
			O OR Killed Wounded Missing
			       O OR O OR O OR
			4 276 6 3 - 83 1 184
			Officers Casualties. Wounded
			CAPT L H RENDELL
			Lieut F J M GRIFFITHS
			2/Lieut W FORD. Gassed 2/Lt RE GREETHEAD
				Sd.

do	24/7/18		The day passed quietly no active operations taking place but Enemy heavily shelled area during day. Positions were further consolidated during day. The right passed quietly. The front was actively patrolled. Posts Established connecting left flank with RIGHT FRENCH FLANK.
			
			Casualties Killed Wounded Missing Wounded(Gas)
			     O OR O OR O OR O OR
			     - 25 5 - 1 - - 19
				Sd.

Army Form C. 2118.

WAR DIARY
or
INTELLIGENCE SUMMARY.
(Erase heading not required.)

Place	Date	Hour	Summary of Events and Information	Remarks and references to Appendices
OULCHY LE CHATEAU	25/7/18	06.00	Our Barrage came down on front line supports and inflicted several Casualties. The day passed quietly except for several Artillery Activity. During the night the line was actively patrolled. The following Officers admitted to Hospital 2/Lt R.L.SHAW. Casualties killed wounded Missing Wounded(Gas) Sick O 0 0 0 0 OR 1 18 - 12 -
	26/7/18		The day passed quietly. Usual Artillery Activity. Casualties killed wounded Missing Gas Sick O 0 0 0 0 OR - 4 - 1 3	
	27/7/18		During the night 26/27 the line has advanced to point 300× West of BOIS DE REUGNY digging in a series of funnel posts of 3 Lewis gps Each. A liaison post was established on the right flank, joint with 1/7th Cheshire Regt, the right proved quietly, heavy rain hampering operations. The front was heavily patrolled without getting contact with the Enemy. Relieved at 11.40 pm by 56th French Division. Casualties nil.	
	28/7/18	02.00	Arrived at BOIS DE NADON where day was spent washing & resting. Orders received to march at Dusk to BOIS DE BALLETTE. Casualties killed wounded Missing Gas Sick O 0 0 0 0 OR - 8 - - 7	

Army Form C. 2118.

WAR DIARY
or
INTELLIGENCE SUMMARY.

(Erase heading not required.)

Instructions regarding War Diaries and Intelligence Summaries are contained in F.S. Regs., Part II. and the Staff Manual respectively. Title pages will be prepared in manuscript.

Place	Date	Hour	Summary of Events and Information	Remarks and references to Appendices
OULCHY LE CHATEAU	29/7/18	02.00	Arrives BOIS DE BAILLETTE taking up position about 817.782	No.
		04.30	Orders received to proceed to VERS SOISSONS Railway in support of 101 BDE and be prepared to operate in Northerly to Southerly direction	
		08.00	Moved to Railway Embankment just West of CHÂTEAU THIERRY ROAD	
		2.0 pm	Moved over to BOIS DE MONTCEAU taking up position from N.E. corner of wood to GRAND ROZOY. All Coys + B^{n} HQ in the line. Heavy shelling M.G., rifle fire. 192. distributes in shell craters.	
			Casualties. Killed. Wounded. Missing. Gas. Sick.
			O.R. O.R. O.R. O.R. O.R. O.R. O.R.
			- 32 - 5 - 23 - 2 - 1 - 1	
	30/7/18		Remained in same position all day. Heavy shelling. The following Officers were wounded. Capt K.S. CHANDLER Capt. 2/L AE EDGE	No.
			Casualties. Killed. Wounded. Missing. Gas. Sick.	
			O.R. O.R. O.R. O.R. O.R. O.R. O.R.	
			2 - 13 - 4 - 6 - 1 - 2	
	31/7/18		During night 30/31 Battalion relieves the 7th S.L.I. in the Paris Line from Northern edge BOIS DE MONTCEAU to about 838.784. In support to 1/1 CHESHIRE REGT + 1/1 HEREFORD REGT. Heavy Shelling during day with Gas bombardments at intervals. Orders received for advance at dawn 1.8.18.	No.
		11.0 pm	Casualties. Killed. Wounded. Missing. Gas. Sick.	
			O.R. O.R. O.R. O.R. O.R. O.R.	
			1 - 15 - 2 - - 11 - 2	

Army Form C. 2118.

WAR DIARY
or
INTELLIGENCE SUMMARY.

(Erase heading not required.)

Place	Date	Hour	Summary of Events and Information	Remarks and references to Appendices
			Month Ending 31-7-1918	

Casualty Return

ON STRENGTH.
        O. OR.
From Hospital - 18
 " Base   3 - 31
 " U.K.   1 - 0
         4 49

OFF STRENGTH.
        O OR
To Hospital   - 46
 " T.M.B.   1
 " Casualties 7. 389
         7. 436

Decrease 3 - 387

Strength 1/7/18 30 - 904
 " 31/7/18 27 - 517

R. Munro
Major
Commanding
14th The Cheshire Regiment

10-8-18

WAR DIARY or INTELLIGENCE SUMMARY

Army Form C. 2118.

1/4th Bn THE CHESHIRE REGIMENT

Place	Date	Hour	Summary of Events and Information	Remarks and references to Appendices
BAS OUCHY LE CHATEAU	8/8/18	3.0 am	Bn moved through Wire & formed up in Ashtray formation B&D Coys in front A&C Coys in rear forming 4th Wave of attack. 101 Bde in front. 103 Bde in support. 25th French Division left flank.	See Brig. Orders. 237/18 & 2/8/18. (Various Attacks)
		4.30 am	Attack commenced. Slight artillery res. Slight resistance and 1 Pr.g. Encountered in wood in Square 183 - 279.	
		7.00	101 Bde reaching their objectives in front. Bn moved out to left front to assault enemy/various attacks.	
		7.30	Bn had captured all objectives. Commanding Officer Lt Col G.H. SWINDELLS wounded. Whistles bring him in owing to severe machine gun fire: the line at the line ran approx at S84 + 9. 809 to 816. 814. Being held by 1/4 CHESHIRE REGT and 2 Sections M.G.C. Le French Division moving up from the rear commenced to file up the line. The line was thinned by withdrawing part of this Bn and formed second line about 100 yds in rear.	
		9.0 am	A fortified about 847. 817. had set on fire by enemy bullets + anti-tank shells, exploding an Enemy Ammunition dump, which killed Capt + Adjt J. HOLDING.	
		11.0 am	Bn withdrawn to area found to reorganise.	
		4.0 pm	Bn occupied Support line about 100 yds in rear of front line Support trench attack later. Distributed in Rifle holes.	
		7.0 pm	French advanced about 800 yds.	
		9.0 pm	Enemy heavily shelled front line supports but no counter attack developed.	

Casualties

	Killed		Wounded		Sick	
	OR	OR	OR	OR	OR	OR
	0.7	59.	0	47	0	1
	3	10	3		3	

Officers Casualties were:-

Killed - Lt Col G.W. SWINDELLS.
Capt + Adjt J. HOLDING.
2nd Lt HE. HOWES.

Wounded - Capt B.W. CORDEN M.C.
2/Lt J.N. HUGHES M.C.
Lieut F.N. RYALS.

Sgd W.C. MOSS.

Army Form C. 2118.

WAR DIARY
or
INTELLIGENCE SUMMARY.
(Erase heading not required.)

Instructions regarding War Diaries and Intelligence Summaries are contained in F. S. Regs., Part II. and the Staff Manual respectively. Title pages will be prepared in manuscript.

Place	Date	Hour	Summary of Events and Information	Remarks and references to Appendices
OULCHY LE CHATEAU 1/20,000	3/8/18	3.0 a.m.	Relieved by 25th French Division and withdrew to BOIS DE MONTCEAU taking up position in pairs tire at 4.30 am. Bn. commanded by Lieut. J.A.L. BARNES. Guns covered in absence of Adjutant and MR HOWIES brought to BHQ for internment. A Cemetery for Offrs, Ranks killed in action was established about B+6. 807. Sund.&Offrs. were interred by the Senior Chaplain at about 8.27. 787. Divl. Commander presented French Decorations & ribbons received to the prepared to move at 2 hours notice. Casualties Offrs NIL. O.R. 3 (sick) Mess. Accounts Sjnt BARJONES. CROIX DE GUERRE	ho.
	3/8/18		Salvage work over recently captured ground. Day spent resting & cleaning. Orders received for move by Lorry at B18.	ho.
	4/8/18 10 a.m. 9.0 p.m	Entrained and proceeded to MANTEUIL. Detrained 5.30 p.m., & commenced march. Arrived SILLY LE LONG & picked up reinforcements & parties from Leave Granted. Capt ROBINSON assumed Command. Ratz re organized into 4 Companies. Casualties Sick O. 0 OR 2	ho.

Army Form C. 2118.

WAR DIARY
or
INTELLIGENCE SUMMARY.

(Erase heading not required.)

Instructions regarding War Diaries and Intelligence Summaries are contained in F. S. Regs., Part II. and the Staff Manual respectively. Title pages will be prepared in manuscript.

Place	Date	Hour	Summary of Events and Information	Remarks and references to Appendices
SILLY LE LONG	5/8/18	6.0 pm	Day spent washing, cleaning up & re-organising. Interior Economy. Orders for move received. Casualties Sick O.R. — 2	Mo.
LE PLESSIS BELLEVILLE	6/8/18	7.0 am 8.30 am	Marched out of SILLY LE LONG. Entrained at LE PLESSIS BELLEVILLE. Remainder of Day on Train. Casualties Nil.	Mo.
ZEGGERS CAPPEL	7/8/18	3.0 pm	Detrained at ARQUES. Marched to ZEGGERS CAPPEL arriving 6.30 pm. Casualties Sick O.R. — 1	Mo.
— do —	8/8/18		Interior Economy & washing & cleaning up Etc. French Decorations (presented) to following Lieut. A.R. JONES (Citation de l'Armée) Croix de Guerre. Lieut. C.J. PARR do — & 4 Other Ranks Croix de Guerre. Lieut. T. STELFOX do — (Citation de Corps d'Armée) Major E.W. MORRIS rejoined & resumed Command of Battalion. Casualties Sick O.R. — 3	Mo.
— do —	9/8/18		Training of Specialists. 40c Bde Inspected Decorated Men and addressed Battalion on recent fighting. Draft of 339 O.R. Received. Casualties Sick. 1 O.R.	Mo.
— do —	10/8/18	5.30 pm	Training of Specialists and Bathing. Warning Order for move to HERZEELE received. Sick O.R. — 2	Mo.

Army Form C. 2118.

WAR DIARY
or
INTELLIGENCE SUMMARY.
(Erase heading not required.)

Place	Date	Hour	Summary of Events and Information	Remarks and references to Appendices
ZEGGERS CAPPEL	11/8/18	9.30 am	Church Parades. R.C. 10.00 am. N.C. 11.30 am C. of E. Rifles inspected by Armourer Staff Sergeant. Draft of 42 O.R. arrived. Casualties Sick 3. OR.	
-do-	12/8/18	5.0 pm	G.O.C. Brigade inspected all Drafts recently received. Day spent training and on 30ʸᵈ Range. Operation order for move received. Casualties Sick 2 OR	
HERZEELE	13/8/18	08.00	am Parades Starting Point where Railway meets ZEGGERS CAPPEL — ESQUELBECQ See copy ROAD, "I" in order HQ, A,B,C,+D. Coys Transport in rear. Arrived 10.30 am 30ˣ Range Reconnoitred by I.O. Casualties Sick 1 OR	Operation order No 1 attached
-do-	14/8/18	5-6 pm	Training as per Programme. Brigade Command x Brigade Riding School for CO's 2ⁿᵈ in Cmd Adjts + Coy Cmdrs. Casualties Sick 4 OR	See copy Training Programme + Sketches attached
-do-	15/8/18		A.+B. Coys musketry on 30ˣ Range. C.+D training as per Programme. Brigade Courses of Instruction as schedule. Casualties Sick 4 OR.	

Army Form C. 2118.

WAR DIARY
or
INTELLIGENCE SUMMARY.

(Erase heading not required.)

Place	Date	Hour	Summary of Events and Information	Remarks and references to Appendices
MOERTE	16/8/18	-	Training in BOIS ST ACAIRE Area. Left Billets 6.30 a.m. returned 4.30 pm. Lunch was taken in the field. Grouping and rapid practice fired by whole Battalion. Bayonet fighting & physical drill. Tactical Exercises. Officers & N.C.O. Attended lecture & demonstration at 7th Squadron R.A.F. C.O. visited II Corps School at MILLAIN, in the afternoon. Brigade Courses of Instruction as for yesterday. Casualties O. S/of O.R. 1 O.R.	[sig]
-do-	17/8/18		Training as per Programme, + Bde Courses of Instruction in Morning. Bde Transport Exhibition reports in Afternoon, postponed on account of rain. Casualties O. S/of O.R. 3	[sig]
-do-	18.8.18	11.25 12.30	Brigade Church Parade 10.30 am. Brigade Sports during afternoon. Administrative Instructions for move to PROVEN AREA received. Operation Order No 23 & received, for move to PROVEN AREA. Casualties O. O.R. 4	See Operation Order No 2 attached. [sig]
-do- Map Sheet 27.	19.8.18	8.22 3.0 pm	Passed Starting Point at D.10.d.07. 11.30 am Arrived PROVEN AREA, PRENTON CAMP Ranges (30*) allotted to Bn. All Lewis Guns fainted. End received from II Corps Coolie HOUTKERQUE & allotted to Coys. 500 to each. Notice received Bde School of Instruction to continue tomorrow. Casualties O. O.R.	[sig]

(A7092). Wt. W12839/M1293. 75,000. 1/17. D.D. & L., Ltd. Forms/C.2118/14.

Instructions regarding War Diaries and Intelligence Summaries are contained in F.S. Regs., Part II. and the Staff Manual respectively. Title pages will be prepared in manuscript.

Army Form C. 2118.

WAR DIARY
or
INTELLIGENCE SUMMARY.
(Erase heading not required.)

Instructions regarding War Diaries and Intelligence Summaries are contained in F.S. Regs., Part II. and the Staff Manual respectively. Title pages will be prepared in manuscript.

Place	Date	Hour	Summary of Events and Information	Remarks and references to Appendices
PENTON CAMP. PROVEN.	20.8.18	6-7am	Reveille	
		8.12.30	Range Practices on 30× Range A&B Coys. Interior Economy, Musketry, Physical Training + Bayonet Fighting.	
		10.30	Warning Orders for move to BRAKE CAMP. received	A/W/B
		5.pm	C.O. attended Conference at 130F H.Q. on 21st received	
		7.30pm	Operation Orders for move received	
		8.0pm	Administrative Instructions for move received.	
		8.15pm	Conference of Coy Cmdrs &c at Bn H.Q.	
		10.50pm	Amended March Table received.	
			Sick	
			Casualties O.R.	
-Ditto-	21.8.18	10.40	Issued Starting Point. Crossroads F.21.a.2.6.	
Ref map Sheets 27.28 1/20,000		2.0pm	Arrived BRAKE CAMP, relief completed. All Officers reconnoitred line and approaches.	A/W/B
		8.0pm	Received orders for Practice Occupation of Alarm positions on night 22/23	
		11.40pm	Received Amended Defence Scheme.	
			Baths A + B Coy SARATOGA Baths.	
			Casualties Sick S.O.R.	

Army Form C. 2118.

WAR DIARY
or
INTELLIGENCE SUMMARY.
(Erase heading not required.)

Instructions regarding War Diaries and Intelligence Summaries are contained in F. S. Regs., Part II. and the Staff Manual respectively. Title pages will be prepared in manuscript.

Place	Date	Hour	Summary of Events and Information	Remarks and references to Appendices
BRAKE CAMP.	22/8/18		Training	
		6 to 7 am	Gas Training.	
		9 to 12.30	Specialist Training.	
Ref.Map. Sept 28 1/20000		10.0 am	Amended Defence Scheme issued to Coys. All Officers reconnoitred line. Disposition of Alarm posts. GREEN LINE South of Inter-Brigade Boundary.	MyB.
			A. Coy. from H.8.a.8.8. (inclusive) to H.8.b.6.10. (inclusive)	
A.3.a.C.			B. " " H.8.b.6.10. " — " H.3.c.0.7. " — (inclusive)	
			C. " " H.3.c.0.7. " — " H.3.a.0.4. (inclusive)	
			D.Coy in Reserve at H.1.b.8.0.	
			Bn. H.Q. at H.1.b.8.0.	
		6.0 pm	Parks A & B Coy. SARATOGA Baths	
		10.0 pm	Order cancelling night occupation of Alarm posts received.	
			Training programme issued.	
			Casualties:- Lieut O. OR	
			1 4	

WAR DIARY
or
INTELLIGENCE SUMMARY

Army Form C. 2118.

Place	Date	Hour	Summary of Events and Information	Remarks and references to Appendices
BRAKE CAMP A.30.c. Sheet 28 1/20,000	23/8/18	6.30-7.30am 4.30-6.30pm	Training as per programme issued 22nd. A Coy working parties under R.E's. C.H.Q. Coy Baths at SARATOGA Baths A.30. Central. H.Q. Amended divisional Defence Scheme recd Cheshire Vol 1 O.R. 3	M.M.B.
BRAKE CAMP A.30.c. Sheet 28 1/20,000	24/8/18	4.22 4.32 5.0	During night 23rd/24th the area was shelled. Training as per programme. A Coy musketry 30 x Range. Working parties under R.E. from 5.30 am until 3.30 pm. Verbal warning order received for move to relieve 1/7 Cheshire M.M.B. Regt in the BROWN line. C.O., I.O. and Coy Commanders reconnoitred line. Addendum to Reserve Brigade defence scheme recd Operation order for the relief of the 1/7th Cheshire Regt recd. Staff of 6 officers and 28 O.R. taken for duty	M.M.B.

Army Form C. 2118.

WAR DIARY
or
INTELLIGENCE SUMMARY.
(Erase heading not required.)

Instructions regarding War Diaries and Intelligence Summaries are contained in F. S. Regs., Part II. and the Staff Manual respectively. Title pages will be prepared in manuscript.

Place	Date	Hour	Summary of Events and Information	Remarks and references to Appendices
ARRIVAL FARM Sheet 28.	27/11/13	9.30	Movement orders received. The Batt was relieved on the BROWN LINE by the 29th D.L.I entrained at MISHION Junction B.27 d.o.2 and detrained at LANCASTER Station 27/F19a95.8 Batt entrained as follows	N.A.B.
B.28.d.S.3.			A Coy H.Q. 12.0 noon B " " " 12.10 p.m. C " " " 12.20 p.m. D " " " Proceeding from LANCASTER Station to ROAD Camp all O.C. Coys reverend behind third over all Trench stores etc. Rifles reported complete at 1.30 p.m. all O.C. Coys & Adj accompanied the C.O. by road to destination via Route A.23.a.4.0 A.3.G.1.9 SWITCH ROAD NORTH OF POPERINGHE ST JAN-TER-BIESIN	
ROAD CAMP.		7.30	Warning orders received Brigade moved to CORMETTE Camp on the 28th Lt. Col. F. de W. Harman D.S.O assumed command of the Batt from Lt-Col. R.B.D Hate	

Army Form C. 2118.

WAR DIARY
or
INTELLIGENCE SUMMARY.
(Erase heading not required.)

Instructions regarding War Diaries and Intelligence Summaries are contained in F. S. Regs., Part II. and the Staff Manual respectively. Title pages will be prepared in manuscript.

Place	Date	Hour	Summary of Events and Information	Remarks and references to Appendices
ROAD	27/8/18	11.30pm	The Brigadier Gen. held a conference at Brigade H.Q. sent	A.W.B
CAMP			C.O.'s March table and administrative Instructions received.	
			Casualties Nil Nil	
ROAD	28/8/18	6.15	Leave starting point at 6.15 AM 250 all ranks entrained at MENDINGHAM Station and proceeded to ST OMER.	A.W.B
		6.45		
CAMP		6.15	Remainder of the Battalion paraded starting point Entrained at PROVEN Station 8.45 A.M. arrived at ST OMER at 1.0 pm	
		4.0pm	arrived at CORMETTE Camp. Transport March Route, two (2) days Staging LEDERZEELE night 28/29 and arrived 1.0 P.M.	
			Casualties Sick 1 OR.	
			Casualties Sick 1	

Army Form C. 2118.

WAR DIARY
or
INTELLIGENCE SUMMARY.
(Erase heading not required.)

Instructions regarding War Diaries and Intelligence Summaries are contained in F. S. Regs., Part II. and the Staff Manual respectively. Title pages will be prepared in manuscript.

Place	Date	Hour	Summary of Events and Information	Remarks and references to Appendices
CORNETTE	29/9/18	A.M. 9-12	Companies at the disposal of Coy Commanders. S.B. & cleaning up	
CAMP.		2-4	Steady drill and handling of arms.	
		4 p.m.	Brigade football competition commenced.	
			Casualties. Sick Nil.	
	30/9/18		Battalion paraded for Musketry on A Range from 5.30 to 3.0 pm	
			Casualties. Sick	O 0 R 2
	31/9/18		Warning order to move at one hours notice to relieve 12th Bde.	
			Brigade football competition continued	
			Casualties. Sick	O 1 R 1

Rowan Kyrn.
Lieut Col.
31/9/18.

Commanding 1/6th Cheshire Regt.

Brief account of Operations from 22nd July to 2nd August, 1918.

In accordance with Ref. 66/2 T.S. of 9/8/18

Map OULCHY LE CHATEAU. 1/20,000.
French System map references.

July 22, 1918. PUISEAUX. At 7.30 am the Commanding Officer, with all Company Commanders, Intelligence Officer and Interpreter left PUISEAUX to reconnoitre the ground to be taken over at night. Met the G.O.C., and all Battalion Commanders at MONTRAMBOEF FARM. After a conference the Commanding Officer and Intelligence Officer reconnoitred the line and decided upon the dispositions of Companies. At 8.30 am the Battalion under Capt B.W.CORDEN, M.C., moved out of PUISEAUX arriving about point 87 at 3.0 pm where the Commanding Officers and other Officers rejoined. At 9.30 pm moved out to relieve the French in the PARIS LINE, guides meeting the Bn at junction of roads about

Relief completed 11.50 pm. In support to the remainder of Brigade. 12.00 midnight warning orders for attack received.

July 23, 1918. Until 3.30 am C.O. and I.O., reconnoitred forward, and covered routes to the Front Line.

7.20 am order to advance received, and issued to Company Commanders.
7.30 am Advance commenced, crossing ground to Front Line in artillery formation with but few casualties, in spite of furious enemy bombardment.

Orders for attack were for 1/7th Cheshire and 1/1 Herefords to take the BOIS DE REUGNY, and afterwards for the 1/4th Cheshire Regt., to push on and consolidate a position securing the CHÂTEAU THIERRY road at HARTENNES ET TAUX.

The advance of the leading Battalions was held up by enfilade machine gun and artillery fire from the direction of TIGNY, owing to the French not having secured this village as was ordered. Our left flank was therefore exposed and in the air and the left Companies moved over to the right into dead ground. Liaison with the French could not be established. The two Companies in front of the trenches East of PARCY TIGNY dug in under heavy fire. One Company in the PARIS LINE trenches and one in the Sunken road North East of PARCY TIGNY, with its right in the village. The position remained the same until about 9.0 pm. Severe casualties were suffered from the heavy shelling, M.G. fire and gas, most of the casualties being from Mustard Gas, from which the S.B.R's gave but little protection.

At 9.0 pm orders were issued for the line to be advanced. 10 pm Companies moved out under cover of darkness and proceeded to dig in. C. Company in front, at about from 00.42 to 00.45. B. Company in close support in rear, and A & D Companies amalgamated 200 yards in rear of B. Company, and in reserve. Liaison was established by joint posts on the right flank with the 1/7th Cheshire Regt and on the left with the French, whose right flank rested on the cross roads about 88.48. The front was actively patrolled during the night, enemy movement and much talking being heard in the Western edge of the BOIS DE REUGNY.

CASUALTIES :- 4 Officers and 276 other ranks.

Killed		Wounded		Wounded (Gas)	
O	or	O	or	O	or
-	6	3	83	1	184

Officers casualties were – Wounded. Capt. L.H.RENDELL.
                                          Lieut E.J.M.GRIFFITHS.
                                        2/Lt. W. FORD.

                        Wounded 2/Lt. R.E.GREETHEAD.
(gas)

July 24th, 1918 Heavy hostile shelling including gas, during the day. M.G., fire from TIGNY enfilading the line. No movement during the day. Front actively patrolled during the night without getting into touch with the enemy.
CASUALTIES :- Officers nil. Other ranks 25.

Killed	Wounded		Wounded (Gas)		Missing	
nil	O	OR	O	OR	O	OR
	-	5	-	19	-	1

The wounded (gas) casualties on this day were all mustard gas casualties from the previous day, the men breaking out into large water blisters all over their bodies and legs.

July 25th, 1918 The position was further consolidated and made secure during the night 24/25. Several casualties were suffered from our own barrage which came down on the Front Line and supports. No operations during the day. Usual artillery activity. During the night 25/26 B Company relieved C Company in the front line.
CASUALTIES. - Officers 1. Other ranks 15

Killed		Wounded		Missing		Wounded (gas)		Sick	
O	OR	O	OR	O	OR	O	OR	O	OR
-	1	-	12	-		-	3	-	-

Officer casualty was 2/Lieut R.L.SHAW.

July 26th 1918
Position further consolidated, coffin trenches being dug into organised fire bays forming series of strong points. Normal artillery activity.
CASUALTIES. Officers nil. Other Ranks 4

Killed	Wounded		Wounded (gas)	Sick	
-	O	OR	-	O.	OR
		1			3

July 27th 1918.
During the night 26/27 with strong covering party and patrols pushed well out to the front, B Company moved forward and dug in 300 yards from the Western Edge of the BOIS DE REUGNY, digging a series of strong posts on a front of 450 yards, with a Liaison post joint with the 1/7th Cheshire Regiment on the right flank. The left flank was in the air, but was held by 2 sections of the M.G.C in position at Head quarters on the northern edge of PARCY TIGNY. The French right flank remained the same and at night posts from A. & D Companies (in reserve) were pushed out to join up.
C Company moved up in close support of B Company occupying the trenches vacated by that Company, A & D Companies moving up to trenches left by C Company.
Heavy rain and thunderstorms hampered operations. The front was actively patrolled as far as the ridge South of BOIS DE REUGNY, which was found to be occupied. Enemy movement was also observed in the BOIS DE REUGNY. The day passed quietly. Normal artillery activity. Relieved by FRENCH DIVISION, relief completed 11.40 p.m.
Casualties. Officers nil. Other Ranks nil.

July 28, 1918 Battalion marched out to the BOIS DE NADON, arriving 4.0 am. Day spent washing and resting. At 4.0 pm orders were received to be prepared to leave at dusk for the BOIS DE BAILLETTE.
CASUALTIES :- Officers Nil Other ranks 8

Wounded		Sick	
O	OR	O	OR
-	1	-	7

July 29, 1918 Arrived BOIS DE BAILLETTE at 2.0 am. 4.30 am orders received to proceed to VERS SOISSONS RAILWAY in Support of 101 BDE. Battalion moved across in Artillery formation and took up a position on the West side of the Railway embankment. At 8.0 am the Battalion moved up the Railway embankment, crossing the CHATEAU THIERRY road, and the right of the Battalion resting on the road. From early morning the Battalion was subjected to heavy artillery fire from the direction of Point 203 Square 184. 280. At 2. pm the Battalion moved up to the BOIS DE MONTCEAU taking up a position in Shell craters from the BOIS DE MONTCEAU to GRAND ROZOY, to fill the gap caused by the French withdrawal on our left. Shell fire very heavy. Enemy seen in large numbers on the ridge East of GRAND ROZOY, and engaged with long range Lewis and Machine gun fire. Enemy snipers established themselves in GRAND ROZOY and Machine guns in the woods East of the Village. The

July 29th (Continued).

The Battalion remained in this position all day.
CASUALTIES :- Officers 1. Other ranks 32

Killed		Wounded		Missing		Wounded (gas)		Sick	
O	OR	O	OR	O	OR	O	OR	O	OR
-	5	1	23	-	2	-	1	-	1

The Officer wounded was 2/Lieut H.C.CALDERWOOD.

July 30, 1918
Battalion remained in the same position all day under heavy shell fire.
CASUALTIES. 2 Officers 13 Other ranks.

Killed		Wounded		Wounded (gas)		Sick	
O	OR	O	OR	O	OR	O	OR
-	4	2	6	-	1	-	2

Officers wounded were - Capt K.S.CHANDLER.
2/Lt.A.E.EDGE.

July 31st, 1918
During the night 30/31 the Battalion relieved the 2/4 S.L.I. in the PARIS LINE from the Northern edge of the BOIS DE MONTCEAU to about 838.784 coming into support of the 1/7th Cheshire Regt. and 1/1 Hereford Regt who held a line of coffin trenches about 600 yards in front. Heavy shelling and gas bombardments at intervals. At 11. 0 p.m., orders for the advance at dawn, 1/8/18 were received.
CASUALTIES. Officers nil Other ranks 15.

Killed		Wounded (gas)		Sick	
O	OR	O	OR	O	OR
-	2	-	11	-	2

August 1st, 1918
At 4. 0 am the Battalion moved through the wire and formed up for the attack in accordance with operation orders received the previous night. The battalions was organised into 5 platoons, B. & D. Companies, and A & C in support, in artillery formation, forming the 4th wave of the attack. The 101 BDE was in front, the 103 BDE on the Right Flank and the 25th French Division on the left. The advance commenced about 4. 30 am under slight artillery fire, Some resistance was encountered in the wood in Square 183 - 279 Just North of the GRAND ROZOY - BEUGNEUX ROAD. The 101 BDE captured and held their objectives by 7. 0 am, and the Battalion moving out to the left front assaulted and took all objectives by 7. 30 am. About this time the Commanding Officer, Lieut Col G.H.SWINDELLS was seen to fall, but owing to severe machine gun fire covering the area, several attempts made to bring him in only resulted in casualties. At this time the line ran approximately 849.809 to 846.814. This line was very strongly held by the 1/4 Bn The Cheshire Regiment, the M.G. Sections attached and also the French Infantry, who had commenced filling up the line from the rear. About 9. 0 am a cornfield about 847. 812 was set on fire by tracer bullets and anti-tank shells and an enemy ammunition dump, killing Capt & Adjt J. HOLDING, and several Other Ranks. The line was thinned by withdrawing part of this Battalion, and a support line formed 100 yards in rear. At 11. 0 am as the French continued to fill up the line, the Battalion was withdrawn entirely to dead ground about 200 yards in rear of the front line, to reorganise; this position was occupied until about 3. 30 pm. In the meantime Signal Communication had been established with the 101 BDE, and 102 BDE. Liaison was established with the 25th French Division on the left. At 3. 30 pm the French requested the Battalion to occupy the second line, 400 yards in rear of the front line, to support their attack at 7. 0 p.m. This was done at 4. 0 pm., the Battalion occupying a series of shell craters. The French advanced about 500 yards at 7. 0 pm and the enemy heavily shelled the front line and supports at 9. 0 pm, but no counter attack developed.

CASUALTIES. Officers 7 Other ranks 59

Killed		Wounded		Missing		Wounded(gas)		Sick	
O	OR	O	OR	O	OR	O	OR	O	OR
3	10	3	42	-	3	1	3	-	1

Officers casualties. Killed. Lt.Col G.H.SWINDELLS.
Capt & Adjt J. HOLDING. Wounded(gas)
Lieut H.E.HOWES. 2/Lt C.MOSS
Wounded. Capt B.W.CORDEN M.C. Lieut F.N.RYALLS
2/Lt J.N.HUGHES

August 2nd, 1918. At 3.0 am the 25th French Division relived the Battalion and a position in the PARIS LINE at the BOIS DE MONTCEAU was occupied by the Battalion at 4.30 am. The day was spent washing and cleaning. Salvage work was carried out over the area covered by the Battalion during the advance the previous day.; the dead were buried, a cemetery being established at about 846.807. The bodies of Lt.Col G.H.SWINDELLS, Capt & Adjt J. HOLDING and Lieut H.E.HOWES were brought in and buried by the Senior C.F., at about 827,787. Salvage work was also carried out in the BOIS DE MONTCEAU and the area covered by the advance on the 29th.

CASUALTIES. Officers nil. Other ranks 3. (sick).

                Major.
    Commanding
    1/4th Bn CHESHIRE REGIMENT.

12. 8. 1918

Copy No 2   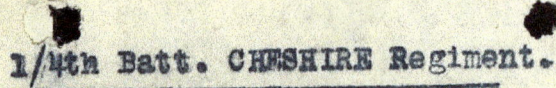   Operation ORDER. No.1.

12.8.15.

Ref. Map.
Sheet 27 1/40.000.

....

1. The 102nd Infantry Brigade will move to HERZEELE Area tomorrow, the 13th instant in the following order:-
    1. 102nd Infantry Brigade H.Q.
    2. 102nd L.T.M.B.
    3. 1/4th Bn. Cheshire Regt.
    4. 1/7th Bn. Cheshire Regt.
    5. 1/1st Bn. Hereford Regt.
    6. No 3. Train.

2. Head of the column will pass starting point, BATTALION ORDERLY ROOM at 7.55 a.m. in the following order:-

    H.Q. A. B. C. D. Coys, Transport.

3. Intervals as given in Brigade letter T.S. 67/1 of 2nd ultimo, circulated xxx tonight, will be observed.

4. Transport and Headquarters will move in accordance with TS 67/9 of 12th ult, attached.

5. Steel helmets will be carried on the back of the pack under the cross straps.
   Mess tins will be carried as described in confidential letter to O.C. Coys today.

6. Advance parties and Billet guides have proceeded to new Area today.

7. Acknowledge receipt.

12.8.15.

Herbert Warner. 2nd/Lieut
A/Adjutant, 1/4th Batt. Cheshire Regt

DISTRIBUTION.
1. C.O.
2. Adjt.
3. A.coy.
4. B. "
5. C. "
6. D. "
7. T.O.
8. I.O.
9. Q.M.
10. War diaries.
11. File

Issued at 8.p.m.

COPY NO....   SECRET.

1/4th BATTALION THE CHESHIRE REGIMENT OPERATION ORDER No. 2.

18th AUGUST 1917.

Reference Map.
Sheet 27 1/40,000.

1. The 102nd Infantry Brigade will move to PROVEN AREA tomorrow the 19th in the following order:-
   1. 102nd Infantry Brigade H.Q.
   2. 102nd L.T.M.B.
   3. 1/7th Cheshire Regiment.
   4. 1/4th Bn. The Cheshire Regiment.
   5. 1/1st Hereford Regiment.
   6. No 3 Train, A.S.C.
   On the 21st instant the Brigade will move to the Reserve Area 49th Division in relief of the 148th Infantry Brigade. Detailed orders will be issued later.

2. Head of the Column will pass the starting point BATTALION Orderly Room at 8.15 am tomorrow in the order:- H.Q., B, C, D, & A Coys, Transport.

3. Usual intervals will be strictly maintained during the whole march. Column will halt at 10 minutes to the clock hour.

4. Transport and Headquarters will move in accordance with T.S.47/9 of 15th ultimo issued with Operation Order No 1.

5. Steel Helmets will be carried on the back of the pack under the cross straps, with the Chequer Badge uppermost. Mess tins will be carried by the handle, supported by the short vertical straps. Iron rations will be carried inside the packs.

6. Advance parties and Billet guides have proceeded to new area to-day.

7. Officers kits will be dumped at Transport Lines at 6.30 am tomorrow morning.

8. Sector Commandants and Guides in relief of similar parties of 147th Brigade will be detailed by the Battalion as follows:-

	N.C.Os	PTEs.
CHEQUER LINE (VLAMERTINGHE)		
YELLOW LINE (BRANDHOEK)	1	6
	1	12

Relief will be carried out on the 19th inst. Full details will be issued later. Outgoing Commandants and Guides will remain in their respective lines for 24 hours before relief. All lines, dispositions, maps and schemes will be carefully taken over.

9. Acknowledge receipt.

2/Lieut.
A/Adjutant, 1/4th Bn. The Cheshire Regiment.

Distribution:-
1 - C.O.
2 - Adjutant.
3 - Captain J.E.DANGER.
4 - O.C. "A" Coy.
5 - O.C. "B" Coy.
6 - O.C. "C" Coy.
7 - O.C. "D" Coy.
8 - Transport Officer
9 - Intelligence Officer.
10 - Quartermaster.
11 - War Diary.
12 - do
13 - O.C. H.Q.
14 - File.

Army Form C. 2118.

WAR DIARY
INTELLIGENCE SUMMARY.
(Erase heading not required.)

Instructions regarding War Diaries and Intelligence Summaries are contained in F.S. Regs., Part II. and the Staff Manual respectively. Title pages will be prepared in manuscript.

1/4 Cheshire Vol 4

Place	Date	Hour	Summary of Events and Information	Remarks and references to Appendices
Tournehem	1/9/18	8.0am	Reference Map 28.SW2 1:20.000. Standing by ready to move.	Nil
		2 pm	Marched out of camp & proceeded to LUMBRES where to entrain.	
LUMBRES	do	4.30pm	Entrained, proceeded to ABEELE arrived there 12 midnight.	Nil
		9.30 am	Regimental transports left CORNETTE 9.30 am for two days trek.	
	do	12 Midt	ABEELE Battalion moved from ABEELE on route to SCHERPENBERG.	
SCHERPENBERG	2/9	4 am	Arrived SCHERPENBERG and relieved B. & I. Leicesters.	Nil
	do	4 pm	Orders received from 102 Inf. Bde. To move and reoccupy line VIERSTRAAT APP I	
	do	12 Mid	SWITCH in relief of 103 Inf. Bde. SWITCH relief completed.	VIERSTRAAT SWITCH TRENCH
VIERSTRAAT SWITCH	3/9	0 am	Position occupied by Companies as follows: VIERSTRAAT SWITCH TRENCH	(Scorrible)
			A. RAMILLES CAMP 28 N 2ya to 28 N 22 a 83	
			B. do 28 N 2ya to 28 N 2y d 52	
			C. L range at 28 N 2y a 54	
			D. 28 N 2y d 52 to 28 N 13 d 72	
			Battalion HQ N.W.9 KEMMEL CHURCH	
			2/Lieut BIDDULPH killed during night 2-3.IX.18	
	do	12 mid	Artillery received from 102 Inf. Bde. to … this morning to support of BECKWITH CRATERS	APP II
			Hy Chps. and 1/1 Herefords who were to take over position relieved with Wilt. & Rifle.	

WAR DIARY
INTELLIGENCE SUMMARY

(Erase heading not required.)

Army Form C. 2118.

Instructions regarding War Diaries and Intelligence Summaries are contained in F. S. Regs., Part II. and the Staff Manual respectively. Title pages will be prepared in manuscript.

Place	Date	Hour	Summary of Events and Information	Remarks and references to Appendices
VIERSTRAAT SWITCH	3/4/		To Attack and take WYTSCHAETE.	Officers Wounded 1 2nd Lt Killed 1 2nd Lt Wounded 1 O.R. Killed 6 O.R. Wounded 29 O.R. Gassed 3 O.R. Missing 16
do	4/4/	4.30am	Battalion formed up at 28 N 2y d 52 ready to move. Casualties during advance : Lieut D.M. RIGBY killed, Lieut G.R. MONTAGUE, M.C., wounded, 2nd Lieut CORLETT wounded.	
		4.30pm		
do	do	4.30am 4.30pm	Battalion held up at 28 N 29 d and d. Lt Col F. de W. HARMAN evacuated sick. Capt Damon assumed command of Battalion. Orders received from 102 Inf Bde to attack HARSAM and PECKHAM CRATERS on ridge 28N30a.	APP III feb.
5/4/	3.15am		Bomb D Coys advance to attack.	
do	4.30am		Major O.E.H. MORRIS took over Command 9th Battalion from CAPT DAWSON. Attack held up by wire and machine gun fire at close range.	APP IV O.R. Killed 1 O.R. Wounded 9
do	7am		Positions reach by (S)? No under:- A. 28 N 29 d 4 2 to 28 N 29 d y 5 D (in reserve) 28 N 29 d 12.18 to 28 N 29 d 10 95 B. 28 N 29 d 3 2 to 28 N 29 d 3 4 about 28N29 d 6 9. C. 28 N 29 Battn HQ. 25 N 20 d 25 Lieut Humphreys Killed	do.
do	2pm		Orders received from 102 Inf Bde for 1/6 Royal Inniskilling O.T.R. relieve this Battalion. Relief completed; trenches etc. taken over from 28 N 2 y c to 28 N 22 a 5 2. Orders received from 102 Inf Bde for change of boundary.	APP V
VIERSTRAAT SWITCH	6/4/	12 mid.		APP VI Officers Wounded 1 O.R. Killed 1 Wounded 50
do	7/4/		Moves to new area during night 7–8/4/18. Position P(?) : A. 28 N 22 a 9 8 to 28 N 22 a 11 B. 28 N 16 d 4 3 to 28 N 22 a 9 8 C. 28 N ~~H~~ to 28 N 16 d 4 3 D. 28 N 14 a 4 4 to 28 N Yc 9 0 95 14 c 90 95 Battn H.Q. SIEGE FARM 28 N 16 c 26 90	

Army Form C. 2118.

WAR DIARY
INTELLIGENCE SUMMARY.
(Erase heading not required.)

Instructions regarding War Diaries and Intelligence Summaries are contained in F.S. Regs., Part II. and the Staff Manual respectively. Title pages will be prepared in manuscript.

Place	Date	Hour	Summary of Events and Information	Remarks and references to Appendices
	9/4/ to	12 m.d.	Orders for relief received from 102 Inf Bde. Relief completed. Positions q/Coy:- A. BERMUDA SUPPORT 28 M 12 d B. SCHERPENBERG - DICKEBUSCH LAKE Line 28 M 12 d C. BERMUDA SUPPORT PRECIPICE RESERVE BERMUDA TRENCH 26 M 12 d and 28 N Y C D. PRECIPICE SUPPORT 28 M 18 L Batt. H.Q. 28 M 12 d 4840.	APP VII Casualties N/L Nil
SCHERPENBERG	10/4/	9.30 a.m 12.30 p.m	Company training carried on:- Gas, P.&B.T., Musketry, Signalling, &combt. Inspection of Lewis Guns by Commanding Officer. Lieut Evans Ockle reported for duty.	Casualties N/L Nil
do	11/4/		Training carried on but interfered with by rain. Honours awarded: To J.M.C.&C. as under:- Bar to Military Cross: Capt. F.C. Murphy M.C. Capt. 10.2 Riddle R.A.M.C. att'd 1/4 Cheshire R.R. Military Medals: 200 238 Sgt. F. Rice 200 204 " W.E. Rogers 200 676 Pte S.Atkinson 40194 Cpl. F. Horan 201570 " W.T. Easton 200488 Pte. F.S. Minor 200904 " F. Orrivan 200 890 " 200 908 " E.H. Jones # Evans	Casualties N/L Nil

Army Form C. 2118.

WAR DIARY
INTELLIGENCE SUMMARY.
(Erase heading not required.)

Place	Date	Hour	Summary of Events and Information	Casualties	Remarks and references to Appendices
SCHERPENBERG	12/1/4		Raining continued as previous day	NIL	Nil
do	13/1/4		Capt A Brown & Infantin Rft. transports received from 102 Inf Bn.	NIL	App VIII Nil
do	14/1/4		Brigade orders received for 103 Inf Bn to relieve Battalion & relieve completed after next reference every Battalion HQ farmer	NIL	Nil
do	15/1/4	9h	Leaving platoons moved off to new position		
LINE	do	11h	defending Battalion. MG (Rifle Grenade) Post at N.35.L 54.54	NIL	Nil
			" " N.29.d 85.12		
			" " N.29.d 82.52		
			" " N.29.d 68.90		
			Support Post at N.29.d 50.70		
			Reserve " " N.29.d 30.05		
			Coy HQ " N.29.d 35.30		

WAR DIARY
INTELLIGENCE SUMMARY.
(Erase heading not required.)

Army Form C. 2118.

Place	Date	Hour	Summary of Events and Information	Remarks and references to Appendices
	15/1/19	11/a	C Coy (left forward). Posts at N 29 b 40 15 Support at N 29 d 15 14 N 29 b 65 46 to N 29 b 55 40 N 29 d 18 24 N 23 d 75 20 Coy HQ at N 29 a 32 46 B Coy (Support). Posts at N 29 a 52 28 N 29 c 58 45 Coy HQ at N 29 c 61 48 N 29 c 86 34 N 29 c 65 05 D Coy (Reserve) Posts at N 28 a 45 55 N 28 a 56 24 Coy HQ at N 28 a 32 52 N 27 b 92 65 N 25 a 40 20 Battn. HQ at Dejreide Dugouts N 29 c 36 30 Capt Fforgue 2/L B. ANGUS reported for duty. Work of wiring posts which were very much in arrear an attempt was made. Enemy snipers active. The left post of A Coy advanced to N 29 A 86.	Nil A.1 A.2
LINE	16/1/19		Inclement. Enemy snipers active.	10R Wounded 1 L Wounded A.2
do	17/1/19		Inclement. Continued to buttress communication trenches and wiring. Patrols pushed out to Snipers scans out. Contact not made.	10R Wounded A.3

Army Form C. 2118.

WAR DIARY
~~INTELLIGENCE SUMMARY.~~
(Erase heading not required.)

Instructions regarding War Diaries and Intelligence Summaries are contained in F. S. Regs., Part II. and the Staff Manual respectively. Title pages will be prepared in manuscript.

Place	Date	Hour	Summary of Events and Information	Casualties	Remarks and references to Appendices
LINE	18/12/		Quiet day; I trench maintained no enemy movements. Enemy snipers troublesome.	1 OR killed 3 wounded	do.
do	19/12/		Artillery effective on enemy: HQ, SQ, CQ, HQ, PQ. 1 AQ shown		do.
		12 noon	enemy effort (?) on Cg Reserve Coy. Casualties 12 men captured.	1 OR killed	do.
do	20/12/		Posts sent out during [illegible] in reconnaissance, during the further enemy advance. Two prisoners captured by L/Cpl Forward (a) Patrols have [illegible] to front of our line.	(2 Lieut Rabelais) 1 Offr wounded 1 OR killed 4 OR wounded	do.

D. D. & L., London, E.C.
(A8604) Wt. W1771/M231 750,000 5/17 **Sch. 52** Forms/C2118/14

Army Form C. 2118.

WAR DIARY
or
INTELLIGENCE SUMMARY.
(Erase heading not required.)

Instructions regarding War Diaries and Intelligence Summaries are contained in F. S. Regs., Part II. and the Staff Manual respectively. Title pages will be prepared in manuscript.

Place	Date	Hour	Summary of Events and Information	Remarks and references to Appendices
LINE	22/11/		Relieving of posts continues. Reconnaissance Investigation. Patrols active in advance of posts.	Casualties: One O.R. Wounded. Appx Ix
"	22/11/		Patrol for night 21/22 Operations Ref annex. Centre of Coy active front: B Coy (= Right Coy) N 35 d 92 69, N 35 d 95 45, N 30 c 25 05, N 30 c 20 20, N 29 d 92 35, N 29 d 60 15. Support Post N 29 d 80 15, Coy HQ and Reserve N 29 d 40 40. D Coy (Left Coy) N 29 d 8 1, N 29 d 9 3, N 30 a 3 8, N 24 c 2 4, N 24 c 45 34. Support Coy: N 35 a 89, N 29 c 88, N 29 a 35, N 29 a 34, N 21 a 45 & N 20 a 42, N 29 c 29, N 28 d 27. Reserve Coy. Battn HQ control det.	Casualties: One Killed. Three Wounded. Nil

Army Form C. 2118.

WAR DIARY
or
INTELLIGENCE SUMMARY.
(Erase heading not required.)

Instructions regarding War Diaries and Intelligence Summaries are contained in F. S. Regs., Part II. and the Staff Manual respectively. Title pages will be prepared in manuscript.

Place	Date	Hour	Summary of Events and Information	Casualties	Remarks and references to Appendices
SCHERPENBERG	23/12/17		Coys cleaning up and reorganising	Officers killed	l.0.
do	24/12/17		Coys. a number of baths at REINING HELST Equipment after battle, and working parties	N/L	l.0.
do	25/12/17		Training carried on i.e. musketry, Lewis gun, scouts rehearsed, and section training. Working parties.	N/L	l.0.
do	26/12/17		Working parties. Lewis Gunners firing on 30+ range, scouts training, bayonetry & rifle exercises continued.	N/L	l.0.
do	27/12/17		Working parties showing continue as previous day	N/L	l.0.
do	28/12/17		Battalion reorganised, 1 Coy A+B Coys, 1 Coy C+D Coys, 50 % of each Coy move into support at St Eloi in turn. Remainder 9th Battalion for duty.	N/L	l.0.
"	29/12/17	3.40p	Battalion moved off at 3.40pm., arrived 020.c.9 6.30pm. H.Q. afterwards at 020.a.5.9. 2 Lewis dept. kept. Bivons stationed upon Brenne for duty.	N/L	l.0.
"	30/12/17	7.30p	Having taken thoroughly Genes Investment next day received	N/L	l.0.

4.×.18

[signature]
1st Lt. Bat. Comdt. 4th Cheshire Regt.

1/4th Bn The Cheshire Regiment.

War Diary

October 1918.

Army Form C. 2118.

WAR DIARY
or
INTELLIGENCE SUMMARY.
(Erase heading not required.)

1/4 Bn THE CHESHIRE REGIMENT.

Place	Date	Hour	Summary of Events and Information	Remarks and references to Appendices
WYTSCHAETE	1/10/18	—	Day spent aiding Checking Equipment and Bomb stoves etc. 3 Patrols reconnoitred Canal Crossings at lochs H.5.1.6. YPRES COMMINES Canal in HOUTHEM Area. Orders for move 2/10/18 received	MS
		16.30		MS
	2/x/18	08.30	Moved to HOUTEN in accordance with Operation Orders attached (No 1).	Appendix No 1. MS
		18.00	Orders for move to relieve Line Units or assault GHELUWE received.	MS
	3/x/18	05.30	Moved to AMERICA AREA, rapid day nothing. Bn distributed in Shell holes CO SO + Coy Cmds reconnoitred forward.	MS
Reference Map	4/x/18	01.00	Moved to GHELUWE LINE and relieved Units of 35 + 41 Divs Ro	MS
Sheet 28		04.30	Relief Complete. A Coy on right about 9 B 25.40 C Coy on left about 9 B 80.20, with liaison post with	MS
1/40, 30 0.			H.O.S.B. H.C. 90. H.O. B in Support. D. in reserve.	MS
	5/x/18.	—	Night H/S passed Quietly Except for several my Retaliatory Activity.	MS
	6/x/19.	—	Night S/6 front Actively Patrolled and Enemy Posts bombed. B.Coy raided enemy post in right b/y front Actively patrolled without Contact. Establishing identity of 126 Regt in front.	MS
	7/x/18.	—	to Bearre. Unusual Enemy MG Artillery and MinnenWerfer activity. D Coy relieved C Coy in Line C Coy falling back	MS
		23.00	Relieved by 1/4 R.W Sussex Regt.	MS
	8/10/18	04.00	Arrived at ZANDVOORDE and proceeded to dig in by platoons. One enemy shell in B Coy area causing considerable Casualties. HQ in P 3 a 8.0.	MS
	9/x/18.	—	Cleaning up, Training, Interior Economy. RE Road working parties.	MS
	10/x/18.	—	Training.	MS
	11/x/18.	16.45	Operation Orders for move on 12th subsequent Operations received.	MS
	12/x/18.	07.30	Further Bn Instructions received.	MS
		18.30	Moved off from Area and relieved 2 Corps R.W Sussex Regt in open trench line near GHELUWE. Occupied same position as on 7th. Bn HQ at Q 3 c 5.6. Front Actively patrolled without Contact. Operation Orders attached.	Appendix No 2. MS

Army Form C. 2118.

WAR DIARY
or
INTELLIGENCE SUMMARY.
(Erase heading not required.)

Instructions regarding War Diaries and Intelligence Summaries are contained in F.S. Regs., Part II. and the Staff Manual respectively. Title pages will be prepared in manuscript.

Place	Date	Hour	Summary of Events and Information	Remarks and references to Appendices
Field	13/4/18	14.40	Night 12/13/4/18. Front actively patrolled without contact. Normal enemy activity with M.G. artillery & minenwerfers.	M.D.
		15.25	1 day retired.	
		18.00	Brigade Instructions (Verbal Arrangements) received. Two hours received. Day quiet.	
Reference Map Sheet 29.	14/4/18	03.00	Bn moved out into Battle positions preparatory to Assault, and HQ moved to Pie Box Q9 b 1.7. A on Right.C on Left Frontline. B in Close support with 2 platoons to Each Front Coy for mopping up. D in reserve.	Appendix No 3. M.D.
'A' 00 00		03.30	Attack Commenced under Heavy Barrage. See attached Summary of Operations	
			Officer Casualties. Wounded Capt R.L.B.ANGUS 2/Lt H.S.HOUGH. GASSED Capt B.A.R.JONES. MBE.	
			" E BRISCOE " F. WILSON 2/Lt C.J.PARR.	
			" C OAKES. " C.E. FINDLAY	
			" F.A. SOTHAM.	
			Prisoners Captured. Officers 8. Other Ranks 128.	
	15/4/18	00.45	Instructions for Consolidation of positions now received. Patrols pushed on through MEHNI and post Established at Cycle Track Etc. See Summary of Operations attached.	Appendix No 3. M.D.
	16/4/18		Night 15/16 passed quietly. Patrols pushed out to ascertain if NAILLUN occupied but patrols stopped by M.G. fire. See Appendix 3 and patrol orders (4) attached	Appendices 3 & 4. M.D.
			B2 withdrawn into support of 11 HEREFORD Regt, which came under Orders of 1 Col G DRAGE DSO Cmdg 11 Hereford Regt. during fencing of Ly's Crossings, 2 Coys Kio B's closely supported and co-operated with 11 Hereford Regt. (See Appendix No 3)	
		18.00	Relieved by 2/16 London Regt. Moved to JOHNSONS FARM. K.36 a.72. Heavy shelling during relief	
			Casualties Officers: Killed 2/Lt E.W.HERBERT. Wounded Capt A BROWNE	
			2/Lt A DIXON.	
	17/4/18		Resting. Washing. Interior Economy. Checking Equipment Reorganising.	M.D.
	18/4/18		2/Lt R.F JENKINS to hospital. 2/Lt S.F. HUNT & connacs.	
	19/4/18	06.45	Moved of 1st Units in Bde Group arriving in STE ANNE area and taking up Billets Nine.	M.D.

Army Form C. 2118.

WAR DIARY
or
INTELLIGENCE SUMMARY.
(Erase heading not required.)

Instructions regarding War Diaries and Intelligence Summaries are contained in F. S. Regs., Part II. and the Staff Manual respectively. Title pages will be prepared in manuscript.

Place	Date	Hour	Summary of Events and Information	Remarks and references to Appendices
Field	20/4/18		Reorganising Refitting Inoculating and light training.	Appendix No 5
STE ANNE	21/4/18		Specialist training	
Reference	22/4/18			
Map	23/4/18	01.45	Orders to move received from Brigade.	
		10.10	Passed Starting point N27 c.8.1.	
Sheet 28		12.00	Took up position in wood in O30c. BnHQ.	
1/40,000		20.25.	Bn Operation Orders received for contemplated Operations, as per attached Operation Orders, but not carried out.	Appendix No 6
		23.00	Bn moved to Area around VANDENHOLLA FARM in O33a with BnHQ in farm	No 5
	24/4/18		During night "A" Companies dug in for cover against shelling. Daybreak quickly.	
		19.30	Provided two KNOCK BRIDGE and relieved portion 23 Middlesex Regiment. See attached Operation Orders (Appendix 5)	
	25/4/18	00.52	Bn Operation Orders received + issued direct to Major MORRIS in immediate command.	Appendices Nos 6 + 7.
		09.00	Attack commenced, "B" conforming with instructions laid down in Appendix 6.	
		09.15.	HQ moved to Tunnel	
		12.00	" " O.36.C. (Winnipeg)	
		12.15	A Coy despatched S. of MOEN to fill gap on right and establish liaison with 7th Cheshires.	
		13.15	Advanced BnHQ established at U.6.d.3.6.	
		13.20	Bn moved forward in Skirmishing lines to final objective as NOTRYVE where it consolidated. See Summary of Operations (Appendix 7) attached.	No 7
			Officers Casualties. Wounded. 2 Lieut. F. ROUSE. F. S. ABEL.	
	26/4/18		Night 25/26 our posts in and around NOTRYVE were heavily shelled by enemy Artillery and Minnenwerfers. The front was actively patrolled to banks of River BEART and posts established there.	Appendix No 7
		28.00	Relieved by 2/23 London and moved to U.1.b. Lieutenancy of operations attached (Appendix 7). To Hospital Capt. J.R. DAWSON 2.Lt HUNT from 1st Army Central School.	

WAR DIARY
or
INTELLIGENCE SUMMARY.

(Erase heading not required.)

Army Form C. 2118.

Place	Date	Hour	Summary of Events and Information	Remarks and references to Appendices
Field Ref Map Sheet 28 1/40,000	27/X/18	06.00	Arrived at W.B. Packs & Greatcoats distributed. Breakfasts & washing.	
		06.30	Orders received for move to STE ANNE to join II Corps.	
		11.14	Passed Starting Point N35.a.7.8; 4th Unit in Bde Column.	
		15.00	Arrived STE ANNE and took up Billets in Convent.	
	28/X/18	06.00	Orders to move to OYGHEM received.	
		07.15	Moved off 2nd Unit in Bde Corps Column.	
		12.00	Arrived OYGHEM and took over Billets in town. Division became attached to II Corps.	
	29/X/18	06.30	Received Orders to move back to HARLEBEKE.	
		09.00	Moved off 3rd Unit in Bde Corps Column.	
		11.30	Arrived HARLEBEKE and formed up on Aerodrome for lunch.	
		12.30	Occupied Billets in Summer Barracks of War (improved), vacated by Newfoundland Regiment.	
	30/X/18	22.00	Interior Economy. Cleaning, Washing, Checking Equipment &c. and Reorganising. Received Orders to be prepared to move at 2 hours notice.	
	31/X/18		Interior Economy. Battalion Specialist Training. Lewis Guns on miniature range.	

J. W. L. Kintlee
Lieut Col.
Commanding
1/4th Bn. Kelfordshire Regiment.

WAR DIARY
or
INTELLIGENCE SUMMARY.

Army Form C. 2118.

(Erase heading not required.)

Summary of Events and Information

Casualty Return. Month ending 31.10.1918.

	O.	OR.
From Hospital	0	130
" Courses	3	41
" Leave	3	140
Reinforcements	5	134

To Hospital 0 99   { Capt J R Anyson.
                    { 2/Lt S E Hunt.
                    { Lt R F Jenkins.

Courses 3 13

Leave 2 112   { 2/Lt W Jennings
               { " F W James.

Casualties 14 297   Killed 2/Lt W Herbert.
                     Wounded Capt L A Angas.
                              " E Briscoe.
                              Lieut A Browne.
                              " C. Oakes.
                              " F A Sotham.
                              2/Lt F Wilson
                              " N S Hough
                              " G Findlay
                              " F S Abell
                              " F Rouse
                              " A Dixon

Killed   1. 45
Wounded   11. 203
Gas   2. 41
Shellshock   3
Lost through   1
Believed K/d   3
Missing — " —   1
            ——————
           14. 297

Struck off strength 3
To 1/2 Th Bty   -
34 M.G.C.   6

Erased 1   Capt/A/ Maj G A R Jones MBE
            Lieut G J Parr.

Struck Off Capt/Maj J Ellis
            " J A L Barnes M.C.
            2/Lt R Saunders.

	O.	OR.
Strength of Unit 1/10/18	40	830
" 31/10/18	29	747
Decrease	11	83

1 – XI – 1918

[signature] Lieut. Col.
Commanding 1/4th Bn. The Ruchire Regiment.

1/4th Bn. The Cheshire Regt.

Oct.

War Diary

Appendix No. 1

1/4th Bn The Cheshire Regt
War Diary
Appendix No 1

SECRET   1/4th Bn Cheshire Regt Operation Orders
                                                1/10/18

Reference Map
Sheet 28 1/40000

1. The 102nd Infantry Brigade will move to the area P.6.D – P.9.O.D. & P.15 to day

2. The 1/4th Bn Cheshire Regt will move to an area (to be pointed out by a guide later) in the following order –

   C Coy
   A
   HQ
   B Coy
   D

   The leading Coy to move off so as to pass the starting point i.e. O.20.c.2.8 (Cross Roads) at 0.9.30

3. The following distances will be observed on the line of march. between Platoon 100 yds between Battalions 500 yds
   N B Care must be taken to ensure that the above distances are maintained when at the halt.

4. All Limbers will march in rear of the Battalion

5. Halts will be called 10 minutes to the Clock hour

6. Route to be taken as follows –

Wytschaete - Oosttaverne
Cross Roads - O.1. c.6.-
O.25. b.0.- - O.18. d.9.5 -
P.20 a 6 2 - Bridge
P.B. d.8.1 - P.14 d

7. Limbers are reporting at Batt HQ @ 07.30 when steps will be taken for their immediate loading.

8. An Officer guide has already proceeded as advance party & will meet the Battalion at Bridge P.13. d.8.1 on arrival & guide it to the area allotted.

9. No rations will come forward tonight therefore the reserve ration at present in possession of Companies will be consumed tomorrow Oct 2nd. Water arrangements later.

10. If a bad turning, crossing or road is met on the line of march O.C. Coys will detail a man to point this out to the Coy or platoon following in rear.

11. O.C. D Coy will detail 1 Officer & 12 men as rearguard. O.C. D Coy will also earmark a platoon to assist the Transport if necessary.

12. In the case of a protracted halt O.C. Coys will practice the men in the working of the rifle bolt.

13. The 2 grenades at present carried by the man are to be carried on the Coy Limber. Care MUST be taken in the loading of these, & each Coy must detail a party to superintend loading

14. Great Coats will be carried & not worn

15. ACKNOWLEDGE

Adjt 1/4" Bn Cheshire Regt

Distribution
  Usual addresses

1/4th Bn - The Cheshire Regt.

oct

War Diary

Appendix No 2

Op orders

1/4th Bn. Cheshire Regt.
War Diary
Appendix No. 2

SECRET 1/4th Bn Cheshire Regt Operation Order No.
   1/10/18

Reference marked map Sheet 28 S.E. 1/20000
and copies of Brigade Secret Instructions
No 2 dated 10.10.18

1. The Battalion will take part in the advance
referred to in Secret No 2 as the left Battalion
of the Brigade 1/5 Cheshires being on the
right. 1/1st Herefords in Brigade Reserve.
103rd Brigade on the left of the Battalion
8th Scottish Rifles on the right. 101st Bde in
Divisional Reserve.
30th Division (with 90th Infantry Bde) on right
of 1/7th Cheshires will attack on the Brigade
right and the 41st Divn on left of 103rd Brigade

2. Advance divided into 3 phases -
1st Black Line 2nd Blue Line 3rd phase is
final objective Brown Line

3. The objective lines and boundaries as
shewn on marked map.

4. "A" Artillery Plan of Attack as per
copies attached.

5. Reference 1 The Battalion as well as 1/5
Cheshires will attack on
  (a) a frontage of 2 Companies with 1 Coy in
Support and 1 Coy in Reserve.
The Battalion will be in its assembly position
with the leading troops on the 6 L (or Cheshire
on map) by H-2 hours

5) By this hour the Battalion will be disposed in depth in its fighting formations. Distance between echelons while in assembly positions being reduced as much as possible. A Coy will be on the right C Coy on the left B Coy in Support D Coy in Reserve. Position as shewn on rough sketch attached

6. <u>Attacking Phase</u>. During the 4 minutes from H-2 to H plus 2 A and C Coys will get as near as possible to the initial barrage line and advance as close as possible under it to the first objective where they will halt for 15" - H plus 28" to H + 43"

1) During this phase A and C must be reorganised in their proper formation. The platoons detailed from B and D (as per attack disposition detail attached) to clear defended posts as soon as their tasks are completed

6) No troops and this refers especially to C Coy will advance near the barrage through Gheluwe Village. The 103rd I.B. are detailing special troops to deal with the village. The village will be smoked and engaged with Thermite shell from H-2 till H+28 by Special Coy. R.E.

1) The leading troops of the 103rd I.B. will pass N & S of the village none being within 100' of the line on the map marking the limits of the village. To do this troops of the 103rd I.B moving S of the village will move in the area of this Brigade where necessary

b.4 (continued)

As they clear the village they will incline towards the Menin Road, East of the village. O.C. C Coy will endeavour to prevent these troops of the 103rd I.B. following behind his Company and get them on the left of his Liaison party, on the right of 103rd I.B.

(iii) The troops of the 103rd I.B. detailed to deal with the village will clear it from the N & S.

2nd Phase a) A and C Coy will resume the advance at H plus 4.3 having previously closed up to the protection barrage line. The advance will be continued to the 2nd objective (Blue Line) as before.

b. On the front of the 102nd Bde. & on right of the 103rd Bde. i.e. from the farm at Q.12.d.95.90 (Jot Farm) inclusive Southwards to the Menin Road; <u>the second objective is the final objective</u>.

The barrage in front of this portion of the line will remain 250' beyond it & troops as they arrive in the line will at once reorganise & consolidate the tactical points in the line.

c. On the remainder of the front of the 103 I.B. troops on reaching the 2nd Objective will re-organise & prepare for the advance to the final objective.

3rd Phase a) The 102 I.B. will continue consolidating the Brown Line (our objective)

(2) 103 I.B. will continue the advance passing on the right about the farm Q.1k.d.95.80 (Jot)

<u>Action of Assaulting Coys</u> Copies of the b.O.C. General Instructions & orders are attached as well as the Action of Support & Reserve Coys (4/1.28)

Liaison. Throughout the advance the closest Liaison will be kept by specially detailed parties in all echelons.

(1) 1/7th Cheshire Regt will detail a special liaison party and keep touch with the 30th Divn on its right and take special measures to support its flank should the advance of the Division on the right be held up. Similarly the 1/4th Cheshire Regt will act with the 103 Bde. Here the necessary action will be taken by OC support Coy should it become necessary.

'C' Coy will detail a special liaison party to keep touch with the troops of the 103 Brigade (names of this party to be recorded) strength - 1 NCO & 4)

GUIDES

'A' Coy will detail an officer with 4 men, 2 of which should be runners (1 his servant) with a signal flag to keep direction for 'A' & 'C' Coy 'A' moving by the left and 'C' by the right of this party.

Re-organisation & Consolidation
Exploitation & Assembly are attached
The Senior Officer present at the final objective will be responsible for endeavouring to carry out these instructions.

Assembly O's C A and C Coys will reconnoitre the assembly positions tomorrow night and place their companies in their fighting formations on night of Z-1. B and D Coys will reconnoitre these areas that they will occupy in rear of A & C as shewn in sketch attached.

Brigade Reserve Battalion

The 1/1st Herefords will probably not move from Divisional Reserve Area until 5-4 night. It may move forward to consolidate the YELLOW LINE during Z day or on 1/5 plus 1 night.

Headquarters

Advanced HQ 34th Divn	O6c 78 Sheet 28
102 Infantry Bde.	Q1d 93
1/4th Cheshires	Q9b 17
1/7th Cheshires	Q9a 11
1/1 Herefords	Q4c 82
102 T.M.B	Q1d 93
(2 H. Bakers Section of 2 T.M Stokes Guns & 23 O.R)	Q9b 85 95
103 Infantry Brigade	K31c 9 6 Sheet 28

8th Scottish Rifles

Trench Mortars Lt Bakers Detachment will work in conjunction with OC Support Coy. They should have 56 rounds and 60 Smoke Bombs. OC 102 T.M.B will supply 10 Stokes Shells of which 5 will be carried by the Support Coy and 5 by the Reserve Coy. They weigh 10 lb, have a 5 sec fuse and can be used for throwing into Pill Boxes. 2 men from B and D Coys will be instructed by the 2 men of HQ who have already received instruction (Cpl Gregg, Pte Ashforth).

RAF as per copy attached.

Greatcoats will not be taken into action but dumped with Bn Transport here under rely/ orders to be issued later.

<u>Supplies</u> On S day all ranks will have rations for the current day and the Iron Rations

<u>Ammunition</u> One tin of flares will be carried per man. 2 No 23 or 36 grenades per man in rifle sections. 2 Smoke Grenades per Section - 25 25 Grenades with Bn HQ Coy. and Platoon HQ

Any deficiencies in Tin Discs will be made up by O's C Coys (apply to Q.M.) 1 per every man in section. Each Section will carry 2 wire cutters and each Rifle Section 3 cup attachments or R G Dischargers. A & C Coys will carry 1 Boche Heavy wire cutters per platoon - and B Coy 2 with the Company to be got from Q M (dozens can be picked up)

On taking over from the 1/4th Sussex in Chelnex tomorrow night all ammunition and other dumps taken over must be carefully checked by O's C Coys and report made to Bn HQ

Divisional Prisoners of War Cage will be at KASTEELHOEK P 7 c central.

<u>R A P's</u>

1/4th Cheshires	Q 3 c 8.8
1/7th Cheshires	Q 3 c 3.3
1/1st Herefords	Q 2 c 80 45
ADS. HOLLEBEKE CHATEAU	O 12 d Central
Walking wounded collecting Post - Plank Road	O 12 c 8.6

All wounded men who possibly can must bring the rifles and equipment with them.

<u>Water</u> All waterbottles must be filled on

J - 1/5 night

As soon as 1st Objective taken Bn HQ will be at Q9b-9035 (Sotham's Pill Box) and Forward report centre at QUARANTINE FARM when practicable and then QUALY FARM if practicable. Runner Route will be from Forward Report Centre to Q9b 9035 (Sotham's Pill Box) to Q3c 8 5

1/4 Bn. The Cheshire Regt.

oct

War Diary

Appendix No 3.

1/4th Bn. The Cheshire Regt.
War Diary
Appendix No 3.

Report on Active Operations.

Extending from Period night of 12th to night of 16th Oct. 1918

1. The Battalion relieved 2 Companies of 1/4th R. Sussex Regt. in the open trench line near GHELUWE. Night of 13/14th Battalion took up its assaulting position behind the line suffering casualties from M.G. Minnenwerfer and Shells. Battalion H.Q. being hit 3 times by 4·2 and 2·14" at 05.38.

2. 'A' and 'C' Companies under Capt. Angas 'A' Coy on the right and 'C' Coy under Lieut Oakes on the left, under the barrage got close up to QUARANTINE FARM. 'B' Coy under acting Capt Briscoe was broken up giving 2 platoons as support to each of 'A' & 'C' Coys, Capt Briscoe and his Coy H.Q. following the Battalion Guiding Party under 2/Lt Hough (wounded) (7Lt Stafford succeeding) as a 2nd or connecting party for collecting and mopping up parties, having runners etc.
'D' Coy. under Capt Danson was in support.
Bn. battle H.Q. at Rouses Pillbox.

3. Assault Coys started off and advanced rapidly, A Coy going off to the right of QUARANTINE FARM which was mopped up by the 2 platoons of 'B' Coy.

4. Sometime after 06.00 round Bn. battle H.Q. a heavy enemy barrage of H.E. and Yellow Cross (mustard and Phosgene) made the atmosphere like a London Fog, with the mist and smoke. Capt & Adjt B.A.R. Jones, 2/Lt. Parr (the S.O) and 2Lt Bardin (Bde Gas Officer) together with some men at Bn. H.Q. were gassed and had to leave. The assaulting troops - as was natural, though passing through but little gas, owing to the mist and smoke, rather missed direction but when the light became better they quickly regained direction.

2/Lt Stafford and men of A & B Coys got as far as
COUCOU, here Capt Angas got an English speaking
Hun to give him information and the mixed
Coys passed along through MENIN Dépôt and across
the GHELUWE-MENIN ROAD close up to MENIN. Here
an M.G was firing down the GHELUWE Road and
another from North of it. 2/Lt Stafford shot with
rifle two M.Gunners who were getting their guns
into action. After going farther to the N.E. as far
as JOB farm with the German, Capt Angas
made his way across to Bn's H.Q.s to make his
report. C. Coy had kept direction well by means
of the MENIN ROAD, but only got as far as QUICK
FARM. 'D' Coy after getting split up in the fog
and going into the 1/4th Area, eventually got
back to QUARANTINE FARM and then across to
TOBY FARM where a portion was taken up in
old trenches running N.N.E. After Capt Angas
had left a Captain of Scottish Rifles told 2/Lt
Stafford that he was too far advanced.
'A'&'B' Coys after withdrawing from 2/Lt Stafford's
post eventually took up a line about
EARTH and FLAME farms. The Scottish Rifles
strayed badly right into the 1/4th area, but their
troops working to the north of the MENIN ROAD did
not reach the outskirts of MENIN till after 2/Lt
Rouse and 2/Lt Stafford.
Some 70 prisoners were obtained about COUCOU
and some 42 near JOB FARM including 2 signallers
who came up from mending the line. A number
of prisoners were rounded up near QUERY FARM
and the huts to its north. One 77 gun was
abandoned by the enemy near the farm, the
gunners being reported captured and another
gun in front of QUICK FARM was really captured
by Capt Angas's fine and wide sweeping

movement along the front from right and left, but was claimed afterwards by the Scottish Rifles. Some German Machine Gunners were killed by their M. Guns. Lieut Miller of the M.G.C saw one of the 14th bayonet 3 men in the trench near QUARANTINE. Capt Angas arrived about 08.00 at Bn H.Q with news of his operations, and the C.O accompanied by the Artillery Liaison Officer went on through QUARANTINE to QUANDARY FARM. Here owing to heavy shelling they were separated and at 08.30 C.O met Capt Angus on his way back very exhausted and reported hit.

He was escorted back by the Liaison Officer and the C.O went in with 2 orderlies, reorganised men of 'D' in old trenches between TOBY FARM and CLOUD FARM and then on and did the same with 'B' Coy who were all closed up in a trench close to the MENIN ROAD beyond QUICK FARM. He then revisited these trenches and found Capt Danson and Coy H.Q in TOBY FARM. A & B were reported about EARTH and FLAME FARM. The C.O then made Battle HQ at QUANDARY FARM Pillbox with 2 gunners. Later the Sig. Officer joined up his wire which was taken on that night through TOBY FARM to A & B Coys.

G.O.C. has ordered up a Coy of Herefords to support A & B Coys who were at the time believed to be between COUCOU and FLAME farm, but were at FLAME farm when this Coy came up and also remained based there.

In the afternoon the C.O. again went with 2 runners and after conferring with Capt Danson with a view to advancing 'D' Coys line to the trenches between QUICK and TOBY FARMS went out towards QUICK FARM.

Enemy opened rapid rifle and M. Gun fire on 'C' Coy and CLOUD FARM. C.O. then returned and asked O/C 1/1st Herefords to send 2 platoons to DUCK FARM to support 'C' Coy which was done after dark. Later in the night 'C' Coy was ordered to advance his line up to GROUPS FARM to align with the Scottish Rifles and later again to point where 2nd objective line crossed the MENIN ROAD.

5. After going to COUCOU Capt Angas had his men along through MENIN depôt to across the MENIN ROAD and then ordered 2/Lt Stafford to go as far as JOB FARM and to make a _____ close to MENIN N of the ROAD. The Bn. left post here with about 20 men or less Lt Stafford and Rouse joined by a 103 I.B. M.G. Officer and an Officer of Scottish Rifles stayed for some hours till 1300 and only withdrawing as a Captain of Scottish Rifles told him he was too far out. About 11.30 Lt Oakes came up the MENIN ROAD to reorganise and collect men but was hit. 2/Lt Stafford and Rouse succeeded in getting away back through 'C' Coy, the Scottish Rifle Officer being killed.
Our post of the Bn. near the gun at QUERY FARM was left in a very exposed position and suffered casualties. It was, however, never withdrawn, or if so it was retaken up by A & B Coys. When 'B' Coy was ordered to advance its line right up to the 2nd Objective during the night 14/15th. Coys were reorganised as much as possible. 'B' Coy on right of Bn. forming up with the left of 1/1st in trenches N of COUCOU. Patrols were ordered out from the Coy of Herefords and from 'A' Coy early morning of 15th but Lt Montague was the only one to get off before dawn and entered MENIN till others did so later.

Early 15th the Bn had anticipated the O.C's order to push out towards and into MENIN, 'C' Coy being ordered to advance by platoons from QUICK. One platoon of Herefords left FLAME farm about 08.00 and was followed by the rest of 'A' & 'B' Coys and later when G.O.C. ordered an advance, an advance – as Battn is advanced guard.
Capt Moggridge's Coy of the 1/1st followed by Capt Poulson. C.O reached QUERY FARM about 07.30 and the Sig. Officer laying the line behind him through the farm over the Depôt. By 09.00 Lieut Montague had reached BRULEE FARM beyond MENIN, after passing through MENIN about 09.00. L.O.C. ordered a further advance to cease and Lieut Stafford with the remainder of A & B Coys formed a strong point near Cycle track on the MENIN – COURTRAI ROAD where they maintained themselves till dawn. On relief of evening of 16th 'C' Coy was ordered to go through MENIN to the RIFLE RANGE Capt Moggridge's Coy 1/1st Herefords to base itself on the MARATHON bridge and Capt Poulson's 1/1st on the lock.
As RIFLE RANGE was also later reached by Scottish Rifle Capt Brown was ordered to regain near Bn H.Q. established near the MENIN DEPÔT, but he was slightly wounded near MENIN before going out to the RIFLE RANGE and did not rejoin his Coy until evening of 16th
When the advanced Guard advance was stopped by G.O.C. the C.O. was ordered to assume command of the 1/1st troops acting with the 1/4th

Early on the 16th, 2/Lt Sully of the 1/1 Herefords who had been ordered out with 3 other patrols, two west of MENIN by A Coy and one each from B & C Coys! 1/1st reported he had got across near the MARATHON BRIDGE, occupied a M.G Post, took the gun, the 4 N.Gunners fleeing. This patrol went as far as HALLUINCH and RUSTY CROSS without encountering the enemy. He with a patrol of Scottish Rifles then returned with men of 103 I.B. a bridge of pontoons was established by pontoons found near the enemy's bank. I thereupon decided to try and advance across the Canal both near MARATHON bridge and the LOCKS. A Coy of the Scottish Rifles did get across with one platoon 200x away in the open plain, but they were unable to advance beyond the banks, suffering casualties from a M.G at PHONE farm, M.G's and Minnenwerfer near the Church. The lock crossing was crossed by planks laid under covering fire by 2/Lt Leech 1/7th. As it was erroneously reported later in the day that the Coy of Scottish Rifles had withdrawn and the new Bridge blown up, I ordered Capt Moggridge who I had reinforced by Capt Poulson's Coy. to reinforce A Coy which had come in C Coys place at the Lock after C Coy had gone to MARATHON BRIDGE.

Here 2/Lt Leech with his 8 mile patrol together with one from the Herefords made a fine attempt by use of local material in getting across the Canal but was held up by the 3 arms of the river. They had their bridge blown up. Attempts were made all the day to cross but the covering troops were heavily shelled and gassed.

I had also decided early to try and cross by the raft the Div. Pioneers had made and which 2/Lt Herbert had left down by the river below MONGREL CROSSING the previous night on patrol. Major Morris was therefore sent by me to direct the operation using the reserve Coy of the 1/1st who were in trenches facing RASCALS RETREAT. He was ordered to arrange for covering fire from this Coy and the neighbouring one of London Scottish. 2/Lt Herbert who was to lead the crossing party after getting them to where A Coy of 1/1st was and the carrying party, was killed whilst investigating the position of the boats. Later 2/Lieut JENKINS was sent with his platoon, the Pioneers making a 2nd Shelter raft from the dump below MONGREL CROSSING one of the Pioneers being wounded. About 13·00 2/Lt Jenkins gallantly led the 1st Party of 2 who crossed in the raft and then with his 4 men established himself on the enemy bank. By 14·15 the whole of A Coy 1/1 Herefords had got across and established itself. They were later much annoyed by Machine and Minnenwerfer fire and suffered some 12 casualties. Only some 65 men of 2/Lt Jenkins party was withdrawn later when the Bn. was relieved, by the 16th Westminsters and was heavily fired upon by M.G's and Guns owing to a light shown by a burning dump near the Depôt. Lt. Williams and a Sergt. of the 1/1st Herefords had been shot on patrol the 14th near where Lt Herbert was killed.

The heavies were turned on twice at 13.00 and 14.00 and 14.30 to try to silence the M.G and Minnenwerfers N and NW outskirts of MENIN but were unable to do so. Before the action I had asked G.O.C. if according to the latest instructions on recent open fighting- a section of field guns could not support the Bn I would most strongly assert that if a section of 18 pd. guns had been attached, they would have been able to silence the points that held up the advance so much and would have saved many valuable lives.

I would like to bring to notice the extremely good work done by Lieut Montague M.C who led his patrol right through MENIN early on 15th and skilfully organised a strong point near Cycle track for over 30 hours and under M.G fire. He is a most capable and good officer.

I have recommended for immediate rewards the following officers and men on A ⅌ W. 3124

I consider the whole great success of the 1st days advance was due to Capt Angas' Cold Cding. initiative and quick and resolute to grasp the situation.

Some 136 prisoners were taken as well as one field gun 77 (certainly) another claimed by Scottish Rifles, 2 Heavy M.G's on sleighs, 6 light (a good number were not picked up) one British V. Gun and mounting and boxes of ammunition, 9 rifles, 25 boxes S.A.A. 3 light minnenwerfers, 1 anti tank rifle, field telephones.

The Casualties were 1 Officer killed, two wounded (2 Gassed) and 163 other ranks, killed, wounded or missing between 05.30 of 14th and relief about 20.00 15th

Lieut Col
Officer Commanding 1/4th Cheshire Regt

1/4th Bn The Cheshire Regt.

War Diary.

Appendix No. 4.

1/4th Bn. The Cheshire Regt.
War Diary
Appendix No 4

Orders for Patrols.

1. The following will send out reconnoitring patrols of 1 Officer and 3 O.R. each.

   D Coy 1/4th Cheshire Regt.   Nos 1 & 2 patrols
   C Coy 1/1st Herefords   No 3 patrol
   B Coy 1/1st ~~Cheshire Regt~~ do   No 4 patrol.

2. <u>Object</u> To ascertain if HALLUIN evacuated, and if not, in what approximate strength held, also if held on the North side and if any new wire on this side.

3. D Coy No 1 Patrol will endeavour to cross the Lys about R.19.a.1.2 and proceed outside or west of the wire to SAWMILL R.19.d.85.30 and on to R.25 central.

   D Coy 1/4 Ches. No 2 Patrol. cross LYS about R.13.c.8.5 and proceed to west side of WEAVING MILLS and west side of PAPER WORKS. down to RECTANGLE FARM R.36.d.04.

   No 3 Patrol 1/1st Herefords cross LYS west of LOCK then past West of LES BARQUES through R.20 central to WEAVING MILL R.27.a.2.5.

   No 4 Patrol B Coy 1/1 Hereford cross LYS in neighbourhood of MARATHON BRIDGE past AUTE CENGE FARM past RUSTY CROSS to a point about R.27.a.6.3.

4. <u>Time</u> leave midnight returning 03.00, but 04.00 if advantage to be gained.

5. <u>Reports</u> to be made in person to O.C. 1/4 Cheshire Regt at Bn HQ Q.18.d.8.8.

6. <u>Dress</u>. Cap, revolver, bayonet, bomb.

7. All fighting to be evaded. Bombs etc only to be used to aid escape.
   Patrols to avoid observation. If fired upon by small post only try and get on behind it in another direction.

8. Rafts are being attempted but may not be ready and patrols will have to swim. If No 3 or 4 patrols cannot leave before 01.00 they will return by 04.00 at latest.

9. Reference above O.6. D Coy 1/4 Cheshire and C&B Coys 1/1 Herefords will be prepared to send out at very short notice and establish posts of strength of 1 Platoon and 1 Lewis Gun each. D Coy No 1 post neighbourhood of LA MALPLAQUET.
No 2 post the RECTANGLE.
No 3 post. C Coy 1/1 Hereford The FACTORY in R.26 d. 9.4
No 4 post B Coy 1/1 Hereford near R 27 a 6.3.
These 4 posts will be supported each by a post of 1 platoon.
    No 1a. about R 19 d 4.0
    No 2a   R 20 c 0.0
    No 3a   R 26 b 05.95
    No 4a near RUSTY CROSS.

Work on improvised Rafts to take 2 or 3 men at a time of the advanced & supporting posts across the LYS must be put in hand at once.
The 4 platoons to be found by D Coy 1/4 Cheshire & the 2 platoons to be found by C&B Coys 1/1 Herefords must be ready to cross the LYS at any time from 05.00 on 16th onwards.
The men of the post will carry Rifles & Web equipment.

23.45
15/10/18.

                    Lieut Col.
          Comdg. 1/4th Cheshire Regt.

1/4th Bn. The Cheshire Regt

Oct
— War Diary —

Appendix No 5

1/4th Bn The Cheshire Regt
War Diary
Appendix No 5

1/4 Bn Cheshire Regt   Operation Order No 3
                            23/4/18

1. The Battalion will act as support Battalion to the 102nd Bde. during the present operations.

2. A & D Coys will move from their present billets at 2130 into the positions occupied by Support & Reserve companys 1/1st Herefords. They will be under the orders of Major E.W. Knight. B & C Coys will leave their present billets at 2130 & after reporting at Bn HQ will proceed with Bn HQ to neighborhood of present Hereford HQ O26.d.3.2.

3. The two Limbers now with Bn HQ will follow Bn HQ, one with SAA & 23 Grenades & flares, one containing surplus Lewis gun Magazines etc. if available, one mule with two boxes of SAA will follow each Coy. One mule will be detailed for Signalling Officer at O.26.d.3.2 to carry signalling gear. Transport Drummers QM Store Staff will, on Bn HQ being moved from O26.d.3.2 remain there until ordered to make a further advance. A guard of 1 man per Cooker & Water Cart will be detailed by D Coy with which they are to remain. Lewis Guns Tools will be man-handled by Companies TO will bring up to O26.d.3.2 Regimental Stores &c in the following order of precedence.
Tools
Ammunition
Water

Water Bottles to be filled before starting & must not be touched without orders from an Officer.
Current days rations will be carried by each man.
No fires to be lit in advance of Bn HQ Gasmasks will be worn at the alert & wherever billeted Coys will establish a Gasguard and guard over retrieved

On the two last Coys of the 1/1st Herefords crossing the canal by the tunnel, Major MORRIS will occupy the position vacated by them, having previously occupied the positions vacated by the front line Coys 1/1st Herefords. He will not however cross the canal until the situation has sufficiently developed i.e. until the two rear Coys 1/1st Herefords are advancing South parallel with the Canal. As Major MORRIS vacates the support & front line trenches, successively B.C. will take their places. After crossing the canal Major MORRIS's two Companies will follow in rear of the Herefords until OC Herefords directs him to fill up the gap between right of Herefords & the canal. B Coy will follow 200 yds behind Major MORRIS's rear Company. C Coy 200 yds behind B. These Coys will not be used to fill up any gap on the right without order from the CO but will be kept intact as support & reserve Coys. HQ after leaving O.26.d.3.2 will next be established West of & close to the tunnel. One Section M.G.C attached to Battalion will follow 100 yds behind Bn HQ taking limber as far as possible C Coy will detail 1 NCO and 12 OR to carry MG ammunition. They will report to MG Officer at O.26.d.3.2. The R.A.P will be established close to Bn HQ and will advance with it. Positions of Hereford Coys will be ascertained from OC Herefords who will also be at O.26.d.3.2 until 2300. Close touch must be maintained by Coys.
Advanced Bde HQ will be at U.3.d.0.7. Signalling Officer will be prepared to carry on the line from the Hereford line West of & close to the tunnel.
With the exception of the following men & arts at O.26.d.3.2 Signallers Runners Lewis Gunners SB's Cooks Wheeled Transport will be used as far forward as possible Two signallers with telephone will accompany Major MORRIS.

Sgnd
A/Adjt 1/4 Bn Cheshire Regt Lieut.

Addition to Operation Order No 3.

1. Medical arrangements have been explained to M.O
2. Stragglers Post will be established at O 26 d 0 2 & U 3 d. 0.7 Stragglers Post will take the names of all walking wounded who do not carry their Rifles & equipment to the ADS. The Battalion will send 1 runner every two hours to collect Stragglers & bring them back to the battalion.
3. Prisoners will be directed to Bde HQ at U 1 b 7 5.
4. The S.A.A. Limbers now with the Battalion will move forward under the R.S.M. No dumps will be formed Directly any SAA is taken from the limber the R.S.M will wire immediately amount to Bde HQ
5. S.O.S Greatest care must be taken of S.O.S as they are most difficult to obtain.
6. Refilling same time & place as for today
7. Reinforcements 2 Officers 122 OR have arrived at Bellegham. QM will send one drummer who will arrive at Cross Roads at H 29 c 18 at 0800 tomorrow to guide this party to Transport Lines.

Amendment Bn HQ will move from O 26 d 3 2 to O 33 a 8 7 from there to O 34 a 2 4.

Issued at
00.15
24/10/18.

1/4th Bn The Cheshire Regt.

War Diary

Oct

Appendix No 6

1/4th Bn. The Cheshire Regt.
Wardrecques
Appendix No 6.

1/4th Bn Cheshire Regt. Operation Order No 4
24/10/18

SECRET.

1. The Battn. will leave present bivouacs at 19.30 to night to relieve 23rd Middlesex Regt. on the front between canal at O 22 central and KNOKKE - KEIBERG HOEKE Road (exclusive)

2. Details will be arranged by CO with CO relieved Battn. at latter's HQ O 16 c 6.3 which is in communication with NAVE HQ through JUPA HQ at O.16.c.6.3.

3. Route via ZONNEBEKE - PONT LEVIS and O 16 c 6.3

4. Order of March "B" "D" "A" "C" Coys. C Coy finding a rear guard and B advanced guard each of one platoon. - The Advance Guard being guided by Lieut. C. E. Allum.

5. The 4 Coys will be under the command of Major FORRES The CO returning with the Adjutant to present Bn HQ at O 33 a 8.7 where (by G.O.C's orders) HQ, by officer & asst Adjt. will remain until Bn. HQ is moved forward east of the canal, probably over the Turnel.

6. Completion of relief will be notified by Maj Morris by the word "BRAST" sent through Relvd HQ, Middlesex and JUPA HQ to NAVE.

7. When the barrage starting point is known B Coy with the other Coys close up behind it will form up close behind the 23rd Middlesex who will be close up to the barrage line.

8. 'B' Coy and following Coys will advance in platoon columns in file on the narrow front between Canal at O 22 Central and KNOKKE - KEIBERG road exclusive The right of B Coy resting down to the final objective on the canal As soon as there is room for D Coy to come up on left of B it will come up with its left resting on the KEIBERG - MOLEN - HOEK ROAD exclusive they advance continues on the left to the east of NAVES and down to AVTRYVE inclusive top (which D must clear) - down to the final objective between DOESUYT (to be cleared by 1/7th Cheshire Regt) and inclusive to them) on the right

9. 2 Coys 1/d Herefords as soon as Bn. gets level with the Tunnel, will follow close behind them and Mop up MOEN following on B & to thicken them on the objective. The remaining 2 Coys 1/d Herefords will follow A & C Coys & will mop up houses etc on the route.

10. On arrival at objective 'D' Coy will get in touch with right of 123 Bde & B Coy with 1/7th Cheshires. The Brigade will consolidate in depth, endeavours being made to reorganise 'A' in support, 'C' in reserve if up in the line. 'A' & 'C' will previously have sent out patrols down to the Scheldt who will remain till consolidation completed.

11. A continuous front line will not be held but platoon posts with gaps flanked & supported by L.G's. They must dig in hard on arrival at objective lying down until the officers have roughly reorganised. After the 2 hours pause the 41st Artillery Barrage will not go south of the Railway Line. The 34th Divn Artillery will sweep houses etc South of the Scheldt.

12. 1/7th Cheshires after occupying BOSSUYT will endeavour to cross by LOCKS to numbers 1 2 3 4 5. and establish Bridge head across the Scheldt.

13. The S.O. will accompany Major NORRIS. The S.O. & adjt & C.O. Asst Adjt. staying at Bn H.Q.

14. Dress without Greatcoats which will be dumped (securely done up and labelled) at present H.Q. before starting under charge of Asst. Adjt. Batman.

15. Half the Bn Signallers & Runners will accompany Major NORRIS.

16. One mule with 2000 rds S.A.A. will follow behind each Coy. One mule will follow behind Bn H.Q. when it moves and one with signalling gear.

17. 2/Lt Leech will report to 123 Bde H.Q. as Liaison Officer at CAPPELLE MILAENE in O 14 a. as the Battn will be closely

18. D Coy will form small liaison posts of 2 men at O 30 Central. C.1.2. O 36 d. 8.2 and V. 8 a. 9.9.

19. Rations will be distributed before marching out. 4 Gallons of Rum will be carried, one gallon on each ammn. mule and will be given out before attack on Major MORRIS's orders.

20. TRANSPORT HQ is now N 36 d 3.2

21. The R.A.P. will be at FARM close to and south of present Bn HQ.

                                                    Hunt
                                    for Adjt 1/4th The Cheshire Regt.

SPECIAL NOTICE

The Commanding Officer is pleased to make the following announcement - 200500. Cpl W. Crook awarded MILITARY MEDAL and wishes to express his appreciation of this NCO's good work in the Field.

1/4th Bn. The Cheshire Regt

Oct.

War Diary

Appendix No 7

1/4th Bn Cheshire Regt
War Diary
Appendix No 7
October 1918

102nd Infantry Brigade.

According to operation orders the Battalion was disposed on E side of Canal S.E. of village of KNOCKE eight casualties occurring while waiting there from 2200 on 24th to barrage at 0900 on 25th. The Battalion was under the command of Major MORRIS after the CO had arranged with CO 23rd Middlesex at latters Bn HQ S.E. of KNOCKE, for the relief and and assembly of the battalion.

CO HQ were first at O 33 a 8 7, then as soon as a message was received from Major MORRIS through the Sig Off who had joined up Battalion Phone with Major MORRIS's phone that he was level with the Tunnel the CO advanced to tunnel, then with the wire on to O 29 c 8 9 Major MORRIS was just overtaken at O 29 a 5 0. Held up by M.G. on the left front he was then sent on in rear of his companies advanced. Bn HQ was established in farm 300 yds W of Wind Mill (O 36 c 2 6) at 12.10 the wire was being brought on here & this was made eventually Bn. Rear HQ. Proceeding further on Pte ROUSE was met at 12.30 wounded, he reported that opposition had been slight casualties slight & that he had seen the enemy running. The 23rd Middlesex appeared to be held up by M.G. fire on our left.

When he left the Companies at 12.15 as B.H.Q. had gone away to the E of KOEN Major MORRIS was sending A Coy round by Southern extremities of KOEN to the right at N to get touch with the Canal.

After leaving ROUSE two companies of 1/1 Herefords who were halted outside on N.W of KOEN were passed through.

C.O with A/Adj Lt PONTIFEX with a few signallers and runners passed through the Western part of KOEN meeting a few civilian inhabitants.

At 3 Uba 4.0 a L.G post of C Coy 1/1 Herefords was found posted. C Coy being believed to be further down the canal. Later this was found not to be the case.

A little farther on some troops were seen about U 6 d 2.9 at 15.17. they were whistled to.

Soon after CO's party reached U 6 d 3.6 7 Lts PROVIS & STAFFORD came up & reported that A B & D Coys were at U 6 d 2.9 & that C Coy was further back in support with Major MORRIS

The whole Battalion was ordered up. A Coy being directed to advance in skirmishing line with its right on the Canal. B Coy on the left of A with its right on the MOEN - AUTRYVE RD. As it had been reported that the 23rd Middlesex were being held up on the left flank by M Gs, D Coy was ordered to advance on the left flank behind B, followed by C in the centre as reserve.

U 6 d 3.6 was made Bn Advd HQ, the phone being brought up to U 6 a 4.4

Shortly afterwards D & A Coys 1/1st Herefords were ordered by me to follow in support of A & B Coys followed by C Coy 1/1st Herefords as their support.

The reserve Coy was somewhere further back on MOEN with Major CHIPP

Before continuing this new stage of the advance the 14th were heavily shelled by 5.9's but most fortunately escaped loss

About this time Lt LOKEMAN D Coy 1/7 Cheshire wounded alone, reporting that the greater part of his Coy had been captured by the enemy about 0300 while trying to cross the Canal, he had been from two platoons B Coy 1/7 & had left them about 200 yds further down on E side of the Canal. I directed Lt LOKEMAN to follow on behind advancing troops & establish a liason post with his two platoons between 1/7 & 1/4 at BOSSUYT

At 13.30 a French civilian who had escaped from the enemy at ORKERDRIESCH about one hour before gave much information (which was sent on to Brigade) about the enemy M.G. line extending from V.10 central - through the N. of Avelghem & through DRIESCH.

In a message timed about 16.00 2/Lt STAFFORD, B Coy reported that he was in a line N. of AUTRYVE with D Coy behind him. He stated he was ready to enter AUTRYVE, but it was being shelled by our own guns as well as enemy T.M's.

At 20.20 he reported he had entered AUTRYVE & was digging in & making five posts, two being near the Church & three beyond the southern extremities of the village. This was done under heavy H.E. shrapnel, T.M. & M.G. fire. A Coy had established itself about this point, about V.14.d central.

D was close support of B & C Coy as support under Major NORRIS about V.9 central. All Objectives having thus been gained by the Battalion with a total capture of 57 prisoners & 7 light M.Gs. Casualties being 2 Officers wounded, 10 O.R. killed and 22 O.R. wounded.

The advance was made with great rapidity over a distance of nearly 7,000 yds despite the fact that owing to the 23rd Middlesex being held up by M.G. fire from S.E. the left flank of the Battalion was left greatly exposed up to the evening of the 26th. The nearest right post of the 23rd Middlesex was some distance to the N.E. or rear of AUTRYVE.

All posts of the Battalion were maintained during 25th & 26th under heavy shell, T.M. & M.G. fire especially around AUTRYVE which was being destroyed by enemy fire.

Some wounded civilians in AUTRYVE were taken away on stretchers by Battalion Stretcher Bearers under heavy fire.

The advance under the initial barrage was begun by B Coy with its right on the Canal as frontage became available. D Coy prolonged B Coy's left to HOSKE-MOEN RD.

Before 2/Lt ROUSE left captured 47 prisoners & seven M.G.s D Coy 8 prisoners. Two enemy were captured by B Coy near AUTRYVE early 26th.

As the rear Coys of the Battalion passed the tunnel, the two first Coys 1/1 Herefords were detailed to follow the 1/4th in close support, the remaining two Coys being detailed to mop up MOEN & the houses on the way.

At 12.30 two companies 1/1 Herefords were found halted W of MOEN.

Had they been advanced quicker & the 23rd Middlesex not been held up, the advance would have been even more quicker & more prisoners taken.

I have submitted names for rewards. I would especially bring to notice the great gallantry and devotion to duty of 2/Lt ROUSE. He was wounded through the top part of the thigh before 05.00, a shrapnel bullet making its entry & gave some Tweedles apart & yet continued for 3 hours to take part as OC B Coy in the rapid & successful advance. When met by me at 12.50 he gave a clear & valuable report on the progress of the fight, though suffering much pain. He only left his Coy when ordered to by Major MORRIS. I was intending recommending 2/Lt ROUSE for his gallant leading of his platoon on 14th October at MENIN as he was mentioned by Capt Angus, but owing to the latter being wounded particulars are not yet available.

I have recommended 2/Lt STAFFORD for MENIN but after 2/Lt ROUSE had been wounded he commanded B Coy with great boldness & determination & is a valuable officer in the field.

Lieut C.E. ALLON my Intelligence Officer has consistently done intelligence & topographical work of a higher order than usual.

Army Form C. 2118.

WAR DIARY
or
INTELLIGENCE SUMMARY.
(Erase heading not required.)

1/4th Bn. The CHESHIRE REGT.

Instructions regarding War Diaries and Intelligence Summaries are contained in F.S. Regs., Part II. and the Staff Manual respectively. Title pages will be prepared in manuscript.

Place	Date	Hour	Summary of Events and Information	Remarks and references to Appendices
MARLEBEKE	1/11/18	—	Battn Specialist Training. Lewis Gunners on Miniature Range. 2/Lt. H. PROVIS to Hospital	
	2/11/18	—	— ditto —	
		20.00	Received warning Orders for move to MORSEELE	
	3/11/18	00.10	Received Orders for move to MORSEELE	
		08.30	Passed Starting Point in LEYHOEK 30th bn in Bde Group Column.	
		11.40	Arrived MORSEELE and took up billets in Town.	
	4/11/18	—	Day spent cleaning up and settling down.	
	5/11/18	—	By Bde. Orders a day of rest. Interior Economy + Baths.	
	6/11/18	—	Battn Specialist training. Lewis Gunners on Miniature Range. Salvage Parties organised {2/Lt R.F. JENKINS from Hospital 2/Lt A. TETLOW joined for Duty	
	7/11/18	—	— do —	
		—	— do — 2/Lt W. SMITH to Hospital — do —	
Sheet 29 1/40,000	8/11/18	21.30	Proceeded Company Bridging to crossing Rivers when in Action. Received Orders for Brigade Staging Practice	
		08.15	Moved out first Unit in Bde Column (heavy Standing parade (Bde HQ) travelling to GROOD VOLANDER FARM (M.10.a.1.7.) where R.E's demonstrated Erection of Bridges with Improvised materials. Returned to Area 14.00	
	9/11/18	—	Training as per programme. Specialist training. Presentation of Medal Ribands by Corps Commander at NEVELGHEM.	
	10/11/18	10.30	Bde Church Parade. C/E.	
		11.00	" " R.C.	
		11.00	" " Nonconformist.	
		20.30	Information received from Bde that Enemy Accepted Armistice terms	
	11/11/18	—	Observed as Day of Rest. Bn practicing for forthcoming Brigade Sports.	
	12/11/18	11.00	Hostilities ceased. Sports running of Company Heats etc.	

WAR DIARY
or
INTELLIGENCE SUMMARY.
(Erase heading not required.)

Army Form C. 2118.

Place	Date	Hour	Summary of Events and Information	Remarks and references to Appendices
MOORSEELE.	13/11/18	14.20	102nd Infantry Bde. Sports. Captain SALTENSTALL M.C. 5th Yorkshire Regiment reports for duty and took over command of "C" Coy. Lieut. CLIST M.C. 5th PARR rejoined from hospital.	M.M.
do.	14/11/18	09.00	Battalion marched to BELLEGHEM.	M.M.
		12.30	Arrived BELLEGHEM and went into billets. (1 man O.R. died on march)	
BELLEGHEM	15/11/18	08.30	Battalion marched to CELLES. A long and fatiguing march and several men fell out.	M.M.
		13.30	Arrived CELLES and moved into billets. Captain L.L.B. ARGUS M.C. rejoined from hospital and took over command of "A" Coy vice Captain BUSHELL.	
CELLES	16/11/18	09.45	Battalion marched to MONT-ELLEZELLES and arrived in to billets.	M.M.
		15.30	Arrived at MONT-ELLEZELLES. A long march but Bn. halted without REMAIN for half an hour in town.	
do.	17/11/18	10.30	Battalion Church parade. Thanksgiving service on Signing of Armistice. Captains BADCOCK and AYNSWORTH M.C. 5th Durham Light Infantry, and 2nd/Lt S.J. O.R. report to for duty. Captain BADCOCK took over command of "B" Coy from Lieut R.F. JENKINS M.C.	M.M.
do.	18/11/18	09.30	Battalion marched to LA PIERRE.	M.M.
		11.30	Arrived LAPIERRE and moved into billets. Captain AYNSWORTH M.C. proceeded to England.	
LAPIERRE	19/11/18		Company training for the day.	M.M.

Army Form C. 2118.

WAR DIARY
or
INTELLIGENCE SUMMARY.
(Erase heading not required.)

Instructions regarding War Diaries and Intelligence
Summaries are contained in F. S. Regs., Part II.
and the Staff Manual respectively. Title pages
will be prepared in manuscript.

Place	Date	Hour	Summary of Events and Information	Remarks and references to Appendices
LAPIERRE	20/11/18	09.00 – 10.45	Company and Platoon parades	
		10.30 – 11.30	Bolshevism Commercial drill under Commanding Officer	
		11.00	Medical Board ranks by Divisional Senior Medical Officer on "Dew Distribution". Following officers reported for duty and were posted to Companies as under:— Lieut E.M. WOODHEAD A.S.C. A Coy Mr. P. SKAIN A " " J.C. LUGG B " " J.H. CHARLIER C " " R.P. HALL D " Captain H.E. BUSHELL to struck off strength having reported to 7th QUEENS for duty.	AM Mo Mo Mo
do	21/11/18	09.00 – 12.00	Coy Commanders Inspection B.Q.C. 107 Inf Bde Inspected Battalion.	
do	22/11/18		Coy Parades + Games under Coy Arrangements.	
do	23/11/18	09.00 – 10.20 10.20 – 11.00	Coy Parades Physical Drill Ceremonial drill under Commanding Officer. Lewis Guns Aircraft Inspected by Armourer Sergeant.	

D. D. & L., London, E.C.
(A8004) Wt. W.2771/M231. 750,000 5/17 Sch. 82 Forms/C2118/44

Army Form C. 2118.

WAR DIARY or INTELLIGENCE SUMMARY.

(Erase heading not required.)

Place	Date	Hour	Summary of Events and Information	Remarks and references to Appendices
LA PIERRE	24/11/18	09.30	HQ, B & A Coys paraded for Divine Service at FLORECQ. B & C Coys disinfected by Sanitation Section AD/VHQ in afternoon. Following Officers reported to Unit:- Lieut A.E. EVANS to A Coy " A.H. HALLIBURTON " C "	MD
do	25/11/18	04.30	1 Officer (Capt E.R. SALTONSTALL M.C.) + 40 O.R. with all officers paraded with Brigade Party. The parade was cancelled, after parties arrived on ground. Bn moved to new billets in FLORECQ, HQ being established in the square.	MD
		14.00		
FLORECQ	26/11/18	09.00	Coy Commanders Inspections. Capt L.L.B. ANGAS M.C. assumed 2i/c Command on Capt (A/Major) E.W. MORRIS proceeding to ENGLAND. Lieut R. PINALL assumed Command of A Coy vice Capt L.L.B. ANGAS M.C. Capt C.S. KINGSTON RAMC proceeds on leave to U.K. being relieved by Capt A.G. MAYFAIR RAMC. Capt I.R. DANSON reported to Bn from course & resumed Command of D Coy. C.O. Inspected A Coy. — D Coy. Drafts of 5-5- 34 O.R.	MD
		11.00		
		14.00		
do	27		Coy Inspections. 14439 Cpl DUTTON F. & 20218 L/c WARD J.H. awarded M. Medal for action in attack on MENIN 14/10/18.	RA
do	28		Lt C.J. TURNER joined Bn + posted to C Coy. A Coy football team beaten 3-2 in final of Bde Coy training. competition by C Coy 1/7 Cheshire Regt. *Lt P.B. GILBERT joined Bn + posted to D Coy.	do
do	29	11.00	Maj Genl STEVENS (Divl Comdr) inspected Brigade group.	do
		18.00	2 Lt E.H. GREEN reported Bn + posted E D Coy.	

Army Form C. 2118.

WAR DIARY
or
INTELLIGENCE SUMMARY.
(Erase heading not required.)

Place	Date	Hour	Summary of Events and Information	Remarks and references to Appendices
FLOUFC_L	30		Ceremonial Drive. Coy Inspection. The following officers joined the Bn. + were posted as follows:—	24
			2/Lt A.L. TURNER + B Coy	
			2/Lt A.C. GROVE B	
			2/Lt F. DODD C	
			2/Lt WM. JENKINS A	
			Lt H.C. HEATH A	
			2/Lt J.W. MORGAN A	

Nye Lt Col.
Commanding 1/4th Cheshire Regt.

WAR DIARY
or
INTELLIGENCE SUMMARY.

Army Form C. 2118.

Summary of Events and Information

Summary of casualties & Reinforcements during Nov 1918.

Reinforcements

	Off	O.R.
From hospital	3	109
" Sources	2	17
" Leave	-	70
Reinforcements from Base	✗20	193
Total	25	389

Casualties

	Off	O.R.
To hospital	2	163
" Sources	1	6
" Leave	2	27
" Base (in accord with G.R.O. No.)	-	21
Struck off Strength	3	-
Total	8	217

Strength of Unit

	Off	O.R.
1st Nov 1918	0	0
30th " 1918	28	746
	45	916
Increase	17	170

	Off	O.R.
Reinforcements	25	389
Casualties	8	217
Increase	17	170

Place	Date	Hour	
Officers	1st Nov to		
	Total 30		
	Capt. E.N. Salkingstall M.C.		
	W.T.G. Badcock		
	Lieut C.J. Surrey		
	B.M. Woodward		
	" R.P. Hall		
	2/Lt. W. Sutton		
	" R.J. Terry		
	" A.E. Evans		
	" C.G. Fairbank		
	" R.J. Gilbert		
	" F.C. Hammond		
	" Ainsworth		
	" R. King		
	" A. Creed		
	" S.H. Morgan		
	" J. Dodd		
	" A.J. Browne		
	" A.T. Barnes		
	" W.W. Hopkins		
	" H.E. Neate		

Army Form C. 2118.

WAR DIARY
or
INTELLIGENCE SUMMARY. 1/4th Cheshire Regt
(Erase heading not required.)

Place	Date 1915	Hour	Summary of Events and Information	Remarks and references to Appendices
FLOBECQ	Dec. 1		Brigade Church Parade.	F4
	2-6		Drill & games.	F4
"	7		Football & debate on "Universal Service for women".	F4
	8		Brigade Church Parade	F4
	9.		Drill & games.	F4
	10.		Bde parade. Practise for medal presentation. Debate on "Professionalism in sport".	F4
	11.		Cleaning up. Prepare for move to VITRIVAL area.	F4
	12		March to CHISENCHIEN.	F4
CHISENCHIEN	13		Rest.	F4
	14		March to SOIGNIES.	F4
SOIGNIES	15		Rest. Bn. Church parade.	F4
	16.		March to FAYT. Inhabitants very kind. Officers billets at the house of Mr. CARLIER.	F4

Army Form C. 2118.

WAR DIARY
or
INTELLIGENCE SUMMARY.

(Erase heading not required.)

1/4th Bn. Cheshire Regt.

Place	Date	Hour	Summary of Events and Information	Remarks and references to Appendices
	Dec 17		March to LA LOUVIÈRE	A4
	18		March to MARCHIENNE AU PONT	A4
	19		March to CHATELET	A4
	20		March to VITRIVAL. Major T.H. KEITH joins Bn.	A4
VITRIVAL	21		Clean up	A4
VITRIVAL	22		A & B Coys + HQ move to AISEMONT to relieve parties in billeting area. 26 men left to be demobilised	A4
"	23		Cleaning up. Colours arrive from England. 2/LT F.N. RYALL joins the Bn.	Ca
"	24		Cleaning up. 2 ages. Notes on parade to mr. Cheshire Innes. 10 men left to be demobilised.	MK
"	25		Church parade at FOSSÉ. Hockey. Inter-coy demobilise.	MK
"	26		Hockey. Games. More men demobilised.	MK
"	27		Drill & games	MK

Army Form C. 2118.

WAR DIARY
or
INTELLIGENCE SUMMARY.

1/4 Bn. Cheshire Regt.

(Erase heading not required.)

Instructions regarding War Diaries and Intelligence Summaries are contained in F. S. Regs., Part II. and the Staff Manual respectively. Title pages will be prepared in manuscript.

Place	Date	Hour	Summary of Events and Information	Remarks and references to Appendices
YITRIVAL and AISEMONT	Dec 28		Parade & games. Look at new billets at FALISOLLE	
	29		Parade & games	
	30		Drill & games	
	31		Drill & games	

1/4 CHESHIRE REGT

1919 JAN — 1919 MAR

Army Form C. 2118.

WAR DIARY
INTELLIGENCE SUMMARY.
(Erase heading not required.)

1/4th = The Cheshire Regiment

JANUARY 1919

Place	Date	Hour	Summary of Events and Information	Remarks and references to Appendices
VITRIVAL & AISEMONT	1/1/19		Drill Games.	
	2/1/19		Drill & Games. Col. R.T. FROST 10th Battn. Corps Commander inspected Battn.	
	3/1/19		Brigadier inspected Billeting Area	
	4/1/19		Drill Games. CO goes on leave	
	5/1/19		Church Parade afternoon & Games at AISEMONT	
	6/1/19		Drill & Games	
	7/1/19		Inspection of Billeting Area by Brig. Greene.	
	8/1/19		Drill Games	
	9/1/19		Drill & Games. Educational "A" classes Elementary French Commenced.	
	10/1/19		Drill & Games following awarded Croix de Guerre (Belgian) Capt. L.L. BANGAS M.C., F.Qr.M. Lieut. CUST. M.C.	
			F.M. ROTHWELL.	
	11/1/19		Drill & Games. Following left for demobilization Capt. FROST	
	12/1/19		Church Parade at FOSSE and Service AISEMONT & VITRIVAL.	
	13/1/19		Drill & Games.	
	14/1/19		Drill & Games	
	15/1/19		Drill & Games.	
	16/1/19		Drill & Games. Exc. By 10th Division Vickers Area.	

Army Form C. 2118.

WAR DIARY
or
INTELLIGENCE SUMMARY.
(Erase heading not required.)

Instructions regarding War Diaries and Intelligence Summaries are contained in F. S. Regs., Part II. and the Staff Manual respectively. Title pages will be prepared in manuscript.

Place	Date	Hour	Summary of Events and Information	Remarks and references to Appendices
VITRIVAL & AISEMONT	17/1/19	16:30	Bde. Inspected B's at FOSSE. Ceremony of taking over Colours. Brigade Parade FOSSE.	
	18/1/19	10:30	G.O.C. 5th Division Inspected Bde at FOSSE and presented medal ribands to recipients.	
	19/1/19	-	Church Parade FOSSE. Services at VITRIVAL + AISEMONT. Form Disinfector at Coy.	
(MARCH 1/10000)	20/1/19	-	Drill + Games.	
	21/1/19	-	Drill + Games.	
	22/1/19	17:00	Entrained at TAMINES for GERMANY.	
	23/1/19	-	Arrived at TROIS PONT and spent 10 hours. Batn. detrained + went for route march.	
(GERMANY 1/100000)	24/1/19	08:00	Arrived BEUEL Station. Marched to OBERCASSEL and relieved 29th Vancouver Battalion B's. C. Coy in Billets line with Wesco Quarters in ROMLINGHOVEN. Bat'n HQ in Villa NÜSER OBERCASSEL.	
	25/1/19		Cleaning up + Straightening after move.	
	26/1/19		Interior Economy Recreational Educational Training. Inspection of Billets.	
	27/1/19			
	28/1/19		Relieved by 1st Dorset Regt + marched to BEUEL taking over Billets of HERTFORD Reg.	
	29/1/19			
	30/1/19			
	31/1/19		Marched to SIEGBURG and took over Billets in prison.	

J.N.Kerk Major
Commandant
1/4 M'gs The CHESHIRE REGIMENT

Summary of Casualties for month of January 1919

Reinforcements.

	officers	O.R.
From Base (all units)	4	54
From hospital		37
From I.B. (list attached)	1	
Rejoined from L.T.M.B.		6
	2	97.

Casualties.

	officers	O.R.
To hospital (to hospital all causes)	3	51
Evacuated (all other)		90
School Musketry (to Infantry)	1	
(to Infantry)	1	
To Senior officers School training	1	
	5.	141.

Nett Casualties. 3 officers. 44. O.R.

Army Form C. 2118.

WAR DIARY
or
INTELLIGENCE SUMMARY.
(Erase heading not required.)

4th Bn. The Cheshire Regt. No 10

MARCH 1919

Place	Date	Hour	Summary of Events and Information	Remarks and references to Appendices
LIND Germany	1.3.19		Lt Col J Pemberton assumed command of the Battalion	
	2.3.19		Church Parades	
	3.3.19	09.30–12.30	Battalion Route March	
	4.3.19		Companies at the disposal of Coy. Commanders	
	5.3.19		Training as per programme	
	6.3.19			
	7.3.19	09.30–12.30	Battalion Route March. Guard provided for Divisional H.Q.	
	8.3.19		Companies at the disposal of Coy commanders for Interior Economy, Pay etc.	
	9.3.19		Church Parade. Inspection of Billets by the Commanding Officer	
	10.3.19		Training as per programme	
	11.3.19	09.30–12.30	Battalion Route March	
	12.3.19		Training as per programme	
	13.3.19			
	14.3.19		Work on 30yd Range	
	15.3.19		Companies at the disposal of Coy commanders for Interior Economy, Pay etc.	
	16.3.19		Church Parade. Inspection of Billets by the Commanding Officer	
	17.3.19		Work on 30yd Range	
	18.3.19			
	19.3.19	09.30–12.30	Battalion Route March	
	20.3.19		Work on 30yd Range	
	21.3.19		1st R.S.L.I. airth taken on the strength of the Battalion	
	22.3.19		Inspection of Companies by O.C. Companies. Interior Economy.	
	23.3.19	10–17	Battalion entrained WAHN Transferred to 1st 13th Western Division (Operation orders attd)	
(ROISDORF)	24.3.19	18.15	Arrived ROISDORF Coys at the disposal of Coy commanders	

Army Form C. 2118.

WAR DIARY
or
INTELLIGENCE SUMMARY.
(Erase heading not required.)

MARCH 1919.

Instructions regarding War Diaries and Intelligence Summaries are contained in F. S. Regs., Part II. and the Staff Manual respectively. Title pages will be prepared in manuscript.

Place	Date	Hour	Summary of Events and Information	Remarks and references to Appendices
ROISDORF	25.3.19	09.30 – 12.00	Battalion Route March.	N/A
	26.3.19		Coys at the disposal of Coy Commanders.	N/A
	27.3.19		Platoon and Section drill by Coys. The 51st Cheshire Regt. taken on the strength of the Battalion and absorbed into the 1/4 Bn. The Cheshire Regt. (51st Chesh Regt at HERSEL)	N/A
HERSEL and ROISDORF	28.3.19		Bathing and Interior Economy	N/A
	29.3.19		Church Parade	N/A
	30.3.19			N/A
	31.3.19		Reorganization of the Battalion. H.Q., Transport, "A" and "C" Coys 1/4 Ches Regt. move to HERSEL. "B" and "D" Coys 51st Cheshire Regt. move to ROISDORF. 51st Cheshire Regt Coys become actually absorbed with the Cheshire Regt Coys. "D" + "B" Coys from a detachment at ROISDORF. (Operation Order No.6 attached)	

J. Arthur Newberyn
Lieut Col
Commanding 1/4 1/5 The Cheshire Regt.

WAR DIARY
or
INTELLIGENCE SUMMARY.

Army Form C. 2118.

(Erase heading not required.)

Instructions regarding War Diaries and Intelligence Summaries are contained in F.S. Regs., Part II. and the Staff Manual respectively. Title pages will be prepared in manuscript.

Place	Date	Hour	Summary of Events and Information	Remarks and references to Appendices
From Base				

Lt.Col. J.A. Pemberton
Major W.F. Myton M.C.
Capt. H.C. Radcliffe
Lieut. N.H. Scott
 " W.F. Packer M.C.
 " J.A. Shelly
 " J.W. Smith
 " E.R. Wall
 " D. Battersad
 " L.S. Pellow
 " T.N. Hilditch

2/Lieut H. Bunker
 " J.J. Harper
 " J.C. Jones
 " H.G. Wilson
 " B. Warner
 " J.C.H. Cottam
 " L.A. Haggarty
 " D.J.K. Poole
 " E.R. Ryder
 " E.R. Earp
 " E.E. Drew
 " H. Woodland
 " W.V. Jacket
 " J. Mayate
 " H. Fellows
 " H.L. Brooke D.C.M.
 " J. McDonald

Casualties

	O.	O.R.
Demobilised 2/Lt E.J. Robson }	2	25
{ 2/Lt J.F. Harper }	1	8
To Hospital		
Struck off Strength ✱	5	2
	7	35

Reinforcements

	O.	O.R.
From Hospital (2/Lt E.J. Robson)	1	14
Base	28	315
	29	329

Effective strength 1/3/19

	O	O.R
1/3/19	31	592
31/3/19	53	886
Total casualties	22	294

✱ Struck off Strength
Lieut. D. Rathwano
2/ " A.B. Warner
 " H. Fellows
 " L.J. Ottoburn
 " W.N. Jenkins

In the Field (Germany)

31/3/19

1st Bn Cheshire Regt.
Training Programme
Week Ending 8/3/19

DAY	0900 to 0930	0930 to 1030	1030 to 1045	1045 to 1130	1130 to 1230	1400 to 1500
MONDAY 3.3.19	Bn Commanders inspection of Arms Equipment	Platoon Drill	LECTURE "The Wars of 1870 & the present War."	Recreational Training	Bathing
TUESDAY 4.3.19		Battalion Route March				
WEDNESDAY 5.3.19		"D" Coy. MUSKETRY. "B" Coy. Musketry applies (30° Range)	Studies for Sketching	"D" Coy. Company drill. "C" Coy. Musketry applies (30° Range)		
THURSDAY 6.3.19		"C" Coy. MUSKETRY. "A" Coy. Musketry applies (30° Range)		"C" Coy. Company drill. "D" Coy. Musketry applies (30° Range)		
FRIDAY 7.3.19		MUSKETRY judging distance		Battalion Ceremonial Drill		
SATURDAY 8.3.19		PAY PARADE		INTERIOR ECONOMY		

NOTE

Firing on the 30° Range will take place, if the range is completed in time.

Educational Classes, Specialist Classes will continue as usual.

W Willm Kant
7/3/19 A/Adjutant, 1st Bn The Cheshire Regt.

1/4 Bn. Cheshire Regt.

Training Programme for Week Ending 15/3/19.

Day	0815 to 0930	0930 to 10:30	10:30 to 10:45	10:45 to 11:30	11:30 to 12:30	1400 to 1500
Monday 10/3/19	Regt. Commander Inspection of Arms, Equipment &	Musketry	Break for smoking	Platoon Drill	Recreational Training	Bathing "A" Coy
Tuesday 11/3/19		Battalion Route March				Transport
Wednesday 12/3/19		Musketry Company Drill	Break for smoking	Platoon Drill	Recreational Training	Bathing "B" Coy
Thursday 13/3/19				Judging distance combined with musketry		Bathing "C" Coy
Friday 14/3/19		Battalion Route March				Bathing HQrs
Saturday 15/3/19		Pay Parade	Break for smoking	Interior Economy		Bathing "D" Coy

Specialist and Educational Training will be carried on as usual.

William Lieut
Adjt. 1/4 Bn Cheshire Regt.

1/4th Cheshire Regt.
Training Programme Week beginning 17/3/19.

Day	09.00 to 09.30	09.30 to 10.30	10.30 to 10.45	10.45 to 11.30	11.30 to 12.30	14.00 to 15.00
Monday 17/3/19	Coy Commanders Inspection of arms equipment &c	Judging Distance	Break for Smoking	Steady Drill	Recreation	Bathing A Coy
Tuesday 18/3/19		Battalion Route March				Bathing C Coy
Wednesday 19/3/19		Platoon Drill		Musketry applied		Bathing B Coy
Thursday 20/3/19		Battalion Route March				Bathing H.Q.
Friday 21/3/19		Platoon Drill		Musketry applied		Bathing A Coy
Saturday 22/3/19		Coy Parade		Interior Economy	Recreation	Bathing C Coy

Specialist and Educational training will be carried on as usual.

W. Williams
Major 1/4 Cheshire Regt.

A/Adjt 1/4 Cheshire Regt.

www.ingramcontent.com/pod-product-compliance
Lightning Source LLC
Chambersburg PA
CBHW081552160426
43191CB00011B/1911